"THE COMPASSION OF CHRIST"

Rev. T. M. CANT   MA. BD.

All proceeds from the sale of this book will be given to the ACCORD Hospice. All claims to fees have been waived, with the result that no-one will receive any financial gain from this publication.

Many of the articles in this volume first appeared in the 'Paisley Daily Express' I write in an amateur capacity. Throughout the years I have always received generous support and tolerance from the professional journalists associated with the 'Paisley Daily Express'. In particular I wish to acknowledge the invaluable encouragement from Anne Dalrymple, the present editor. While a former editor, Norman Macdonald has guided me through the process involved in producing this book. To them, and all in the 'Paisley Daily Express' I extend my warmest appreciation.

Mr James Wardrop, Chairman of the Board at ACCORD found time in his busy schedule to read the manuscript and kindly write a Foreword. While to my wife Coleen fell the unenviable task of correcting my typing. To both I offer my unqualified appreciation.

Cover Design by Mrs Helen McLauchlan

Design, Sub-editing and Production: Cameron Heggie

Printed and bound by Thomson Litho, East Kilbride

Acknowledgements

If I have one regret in my ministry it is the lurking suspicion that I did not spend sufficient time with, nor pay enough attention to, my family. But, over the years, through the years, my wife Coleen and children James and Dawn were always there for me. In these days before church offices and secretaries became fashionable my manse was my place of work. My study was really my office. But my family helped to make the manse into a home. I will always be eternally grateful to them.

During my work and ministry I have met countless wonderful people in whose lives I have seen the very face of God. These fine people often encouraged me, always blessed me. I still remember with gratitude the friendships made at the Paisley Christian Social Action Centre, and through my work in the wider Paisley community. I cherish the memories of the members of the former St. George's Church and the current Laigh Kirk, both in Paisley. The Laigh Kirk years were an exciting adventure when great deeds were achieved and deep feelings created and shared. I looked upon the members of my congregation as my extended family, and still feel for them in this way. They were my friends in a very special way, for they extended the bounds of friendship to ever wider dimensions and deeper feelings. So much so, these wonderful friends helped me to understand and experience the meaning of Jesus' friendship. *'Now I call you my friends'* **(John 15.15).** I remember them with gratitude, and offer to them my abiding love and sincere appreciation. As Paul said

'I thank my God upon every remembrance of you'
(Philippians 1.3)

'To Coleen'

Foreword

James Wardrop DL, F Univ, F.C.I.B.S., F.S.A. (SCOT)
Honorary Chairman of ACCORD Hospice

I first met the Reverend Tom Cant in 1964 when I was visiting Kyle of Lochalsh which was his first charge. When he subsequently came to Paisley to Saint George's Church and then eventually ministering to the combined charge at the Laigh Kirk, he and his wife and family became firm and faithful friends from whom I have derived great support over many years.

Tom's ministry at the Laigh was characterised by devotion and service not only to his congregation but also in an outgoing way to the community of Paisley. In the succeeding pages he has written of the Paisley Christian Social Action Centre and that in itself probably deserves a separate publication. His caring example was an inspiration to many and in all probability the salvation of a lesser number of people. To see him 'in action' was truly a joy.

Over the years he has brought the gospel to a wider public with weekly articles for the Paisley Daily Express and in his retirement from his ministry in Paisley he has continued these articles to the benefit of all. Together with Coleen he is enjoying life in Stewarton and at this point in time he is interim moderator for a church in the district.

It is typical of the man that the proceeds of this little volume will go in their entirety to ACCORD Hospice and, for that most generous of gestures, I thank him, as I do, for so many other wonderful acts over the years. I commend these pages to you having been myself riveted by them and the harmony and counterpoint of personal experience backed by the gospel words is truly remarkable.

10 October 2008

Introduction

'It is the heart which perceives God and not the reason,
that is what faith is; God perceived by the heart, not by the reason'
(Blais Pascal "Les Pensées" 423)

The 'Paisley Daily Express', a local paper with wide outlook, has always devoted one page in its Saturday edition for the use of the local churches. In 1990 that 'Church Page' was so little used that the editor at that time almost closed it. I offered to supply a weekly article if he would retain the columns for the use of the churches. From these modest beginnings my weekly article has continued, and I trust been a source of help over the years.

Many friends (well two or three) have suggested that some of these articles should be printed, and they provide the framework for this volume. This modest volume does not claim to be an academic book with voluminous references and endless lists for 'further reading'. It comes from a tradesman rather than an academic. It reflects the thoughts and insights, doubts and answers garnered over four decades by a minister of Word and Sacrament.

The bread and butter of my ministry were the two roles of pastor and preacher, in worship to be preacher of the Word and celebrant of the Sacraments, as pastor to be with the people of the congregation and parish. In a Sunday act of worship I could recognise the people in the pews and remember the very living rooms in their houses. Equally important the worshipping members knew the man in the pulpit and could remember how he visited their homes and raised prayers in their family circle.

Often my articles in the 'Paisley Daily Express' reflected incidents in homes, or events in the Paisley community, as well as events in the national and international scene. But to the harsh reality of life's experiences I always sought to bring the immediate presence of Christ and the full promise of the Gospel. My articles attempted to be a sort of dialogue between event and thought, experience and faith, hurt and healing, life and death, but supremely a dialogue between people and the living God and Father of Jesus Christ. Let the reader decide if it is a deep dialogue between soul and soul or merely a stuttering conversation.

However, there are two compelling motives behind this little publication. Firstly, over the past decades the Christian churches, and Christianity itself has lost its appeal for the general public. It is now taken for granted that Britain is a secular democracy. Despite the historical tradition of Britain as a Christian nation, nowadays Christianity will be regarded as one among many religions. Prince Charles has indicated that, on his coronation, he hopes to become the Defender of Faith rather than the Defender of 'the' Faith. The understanding and knowledge concerning the Christian faith, the Bible and worship have sunk to alarmingly low levels. As a consequence I have found that I am more frequently using my weekly articles for teaching and explanation. I firmly believe that Hans Kung is correct in asserting that Christians and the institutional church must be prepared to offer a rational account of the faith in which we stand.

Secondly, under the increasingly hostile criticism against the Christian faith, and in my view biased discrimination against institutionalised Christianity by the secular state, the Christian population has become uncertain about our faith. Christianity for many may have lost its sparkle. Perhaps the fire of faith has gone out and there is little warmth in the grey cold ashes. The late John Macquarrie suggested that for some our belief and witness were like goods in the shop window for too long which had become faded. What I have tried to do is present aspects of the faith in a rather more poetic and meditative form. If at times I take poetic licence, I am trying to breathe fresh air into our faith. Only the reader can decide if I have succeeded. That is why I find the quotation from Blais Pascal's 'Pensées' to be so meaningful.

It is not the case that we seek to base our belief on an irrational and emotional foundation, thereby avoiding hard questions demanding radical answers. Rather I seek to describe the whole-life relationship we can have with God the Father in Jesus Christ. As Pascal also wrote, *'The heart has its own motives of which reason knows nothing at all'* (Les Pensées 424). In other words, our whole-life experience is the stage upon which we live our life with God.

The Christian community has been confronted in the last decade by many slings and arrows of outrageous fortune. In my view a secular and increasingly hostile society has discriminated against the Christian faith. But an insidious complacency has weakened the established churches of all denominations. Paper members who never support their church in work, witness, or worship have dealt a mortal blow to the established churches. As Dietrich Bonhoeffer wrote, 'Our easy trafficking with the word of cheap grace simply bores the world to disgust' ("The Cost of Discipleship" page 165). We cannot be complacent. A comprehensive statistical analysis of religious practice in Britain, entitled 'Religious Trends', published by Christian Research shows that by 2035 there will be more Muslims attending mosques than Christians attending churches. By 2050 there will be more Hindu worshippers than Christians.

I seek to balance this religious equation. On the one hand fulfilling Hans Kung's valid request that Christians think rigorously and rationally about their Christian faith. On the other hand, following Pascal's warm thoughts, that we allow our heart, our whole life, to be filled and transformed by the sight and presence of God. That is why the reader will find that many of these articles follow a two-fold pattern. The first part aims to provide background information, and rational explanation while the second part seeks to give flesh and blood, warmth and feeling to the subject by adopting a poetic and meditative style. If I help the reader to capture, or re-capture, even a little of the excitement of meeting with Jesus, then I shall be satisfied.

These are enormously challenging times through which we live. Fundamental issues affecting the global economy are having serious repercussions for everybody. While ultimate issues, determining the continuation or cessation of life itself, stand precariously balanced.

I believe we stand on the threshold of a much-needed reformation in religion and in humanity's relationship with the eternal God. This must be accompanied by a new design for the nations of the world to exist together in co-operation and harmony, in recognition and respect for cultural differences and racial values. The world family stands in need of as new Reformation to understand humanity's destiny. We need a modern Renaissance to liberate the creative powers of the human soul and spirit. And we desperately need a fresh Enlightenment to regain the unique value of human nature, men, women, and children in the global human race. The global family needs to explore fresh ways of living, to create enlightened methods of Earth preservation, and to reach a deeper understanding of humankind's role in this world. T.S.Eliot spoke for the individual, but his words equally apply to the human scene.

> *'What might have been and what has been*
> *Point to one end which is always present.*
> *Footfalls echo in the memory (of history?)*
> *Down the passage we did not take*
> *Towards the door we never opened'*
> **("Burnt Norton" from the Four Quartets)**

It is past time the human race opened new doors. Christians will turn to God in Jesus Christ with our hopes and desires, our questions and certainties. For every believer can also fear the shadow of doubt. But in every doubting soul there are often clear shafts of light and understanding.

We may not possess the wisdom to find life's answers, but let us have the courage to confront life's questions.

Introduction

Chapter 1

"LET US WORSHIP GOD"

WORSHIP

"We praise Thee;
We bless Thee;
We worship Thee;
We glorify Thee
We give thanks to Thee
For Thy great glory.
Lord God, Heavenly King,
God the Father Almighty"

(The 'Gloria' from Beethoven "Missa Solemnis")

1 MY WORSHIP

The following pages contain personal reflections on worship. They do not purport to be a comprehensive study, nor an exhaustive history on this subject. For four decades my weekends have been dominated by worship. Dominated, not because I was obliged to attend church, I have always wanted to worship, it brings delight and peace to my soul. But dominated because the minister's profession includes the responsibility for and conduct of worship. Do the people in the pews realise how emptied the preacher has become after conducting a service of worship? That is why criticism or pettiness to a minister as the people leave the church leaves the preacher dispirited because the service has left the preacher defenceless.

The preparation of worship is absolutely essential. I have never prepared my service in general nor written my sermon on a Saturday night. In my reckoning that is an insult to the intelligent and serious-minded worshippers in the congregation. Again, in my opinion such pseudo-preparation is an indignity to the word of God.

My training included the study of Hebrew for the Old Testament and Greek for the New Testament. I am not an accomplished Greek student but I retained sufficient understanding to carry out my sermon and teaching preparations in the original languages. I always planned my sermons at least one month in advance, leaving sufficient space for modifications and additions as the service demanded. The themes, subjects, and Scripture readings were always printed in the Church Magazine. I used modern commentaries and changed them every ten years in order to keep up to date with modern research and scholarship. I spent the first part of the week preparing the service, and the second part of the week preparing myself. I always produced a printed Order of Service with sermon notes. In this way the worshippers were able to consider the message of the sermon at their leisure. I always wore my robes. For that matter I always wore my clerical collar. I considered it my form of identity. People knew who (or what) I was when I went into a hospital ward.

Nowadays the young preachers conduct worship in so many different ways. Many such methods are bold and adventurous, and are geared to proclaim the message of the Gospel to their generation. New and fresh hymns, different presentations now feature in modern worship. We should welcome these innovations, and as church members support the preachers and ministers as they bend their energies of mind and body to the task of worship and witness. Their ministry take places in a society hostile to Christianity and the established church. The present generation of young ministers must have the courage to break the mould in which yesterday's worship was shaped. Their predecessors must have the same courage to see these moulds being broken. For many church members the fire of faith is burning low and the discipline of worship appears forgotten. That is why paper church members, who rarely attend and inadequately support the church, are a disease in the church and an insult to Christ the king and head of the church. More, that is why I am angry at the diminishing numbers attending worship in church and chapel. If these neglectful church members were to play their full part then churches and chapels would be far stronger.

The minister conducting public worship remains an ordinary Christian in need of the means of grace found in the liturgy. On many occasions, after a particularly difficult week in the congregation and parish, I would stand in the pulpit and listen to the congregation as they sang the first item of praise. I simply listened to their praise. It was their personal expression of worship. Their singing always raised my spirits and eased the distress that I often carried in my heart into the pulpit. Members of the public will enjoy a similar experience. Worship can be a time of rest, an easing of that burden, a tranquil moment in a demanding week, a meeting place with God in Jesus Christ. The same Jesus, who has seen and shared that busy week, invites you into his presence through worship. I have used the following verse more than any other to gather people to prayer, in family circles, at home, in church meetings, and in public worship.

'Come unto me all who labour and are heavy-laden
and I will give you rest'
(Matthew 11.28-30)

2   IN PRAISE OF SUNDAY

When the Roman Emperor Hadrian built his wall across the north of England he erected towers at regular intervals along its route. But every seventh tower was built to a higher level. From this higher vantage point the Roman soldiers could command a clearer view of the entire wall. In our Christian faith every seventh day is a day of worship. That day of worship is like the higher tower in Hadrian's wall. Days of worship are higher than ordinary days, and from the vantage point of worship we can see the whole of our life. Worship works together with witness, in a spiritual dialogue church praise supports personal behaviour, while the events of our daily life can be taken into our worship. When worshippers gather in church, chapel, or meeting house, they bring with them the multicoloured life that was their week. But when they leave their place of worship the blessing of God will go with them into the coming days. The blessing of God brought to them from God through Jesus by the Holy Spirit through the means of grace. Worship is *'The fire on the altar'* (**Leviticus 6.9**). After the next section, 'The Fire on the Altar', the remaining sections are personal reflections on worship. This chapter is not a directory of worship. If the reader can identify with, and be encouraged by, these personal reminiscences then I shall be satisfied.

'I was glad when they said to me,
'Let us go to the house of the Lord'
For my brethren and companions sake
I will say 'Peace be within you'
(Psalm 122).

3 THE FIRE ON THE ALTAR

The dynamism of worship is the meeting of God with his people, the eternal heart of God loving his people who can only live because of that love and reply through their worship.

"The fire shall ever be burning on the altar, it shall never go out"
(Leviticus 6.9).

A Meditation

Dear God
    On the altar the fire of worship shall ever burn
      It shall never go out
We adore you, eternal God
    We approach you in prayer
      This is our worship

We pause
For the ground where we stand is holy ground **(Exodus 3.5)**
Our coming is to you
Our meeting is with you
Our worship is towards you
But you are already waiting for us in Jesus
You are the living God,
The great I AM
In this way shall we come, shall we seek to worship
'Then the fire shall ever be burning on the altar, it shall never go out'

'Then the fire shall ever be burning on the altar, it shall never go out'
But woe are we, we are lost, for we are people of unclean lips dwelling among people of unclean lives' **(Isaiah 6.5-7).**
How can we approach the living God?
Holy God who is clean and right
How can our blind-ed eyes see the King, the Lord of hosts?
For these hands raised in worship have been stained
This innermost self, 'me' wants to worship God
But it has nursed wrong thoughts
How can we worship you, the living God?
Unless from the fire on the altar forever burning
Jesus takes a live coal and touches us to our cleansing
Only then we can worship the living God.

'Then the fire shall forever be burning on the altar, it shall never go out'
'Go tell them what you see'
What has happened to you in this time of worship?
*'Your eyes are opened, your walk is firm,
your soul is cleansed, you hear the Word of God,
your dead faith is raised, you hear the good news'*
(Matthew 11.4-5).
These things have happened to us in worship
Then Father God
On the altar of our soul the fire of love shall forever burn
shall never be extinguished.
Our love for you, Father God

Shall ever burn, shall never go out.
Then our love for one another
   Shall ever burn, shall never be dimmed
   Shall never go out.
The flame of our love shall flicker in the wind
   This way and that, but it shall ever burn
      A loving flame, a gentle fire
   For the fire on the altar of our soul
      Is fed by love, is fuelled by kindness
   Such soul-elements are never exhausted
So the fire of our love and care shall ever burn
   And never be allowed to go out.

The fire in our soul shall ever burn for one another
   It shall never go out.
For

   "A bruised reed He shall not break"
   and a dimly burning flame He shall not quench"
   (Matthew 12.20)
Lord Jesus
   We feel like a bruised reed
      That even the gentlest wind will break its stem
   We are a dimly burning fire
      A forlorn flickering flame.
Lord Jesus
   In your gentle but strong hands
      May we remain unbroken.
   In the great flame of your life
      May we continue to glow.
Lord Jesus
   May we know that on the altar of our heart and soul.
   The fire of your life shall forever burn,
      it shall never be extinguished.

4   THE WONDER OF WORSHIP

A few years ago my wife and I visited Vienna. On the Saturday of our tour we were present in the great St. Stephen's cathedral for a lunchtime performance of one of Mozart's lesser-known Requiems. As the congregation gathered and we took our seats for the start of the Requiem I could hear the orchestra but could not see it. So I stood up to discover where they were seated, and the whole congregation behind me stood up as well. I thought it was hilarious but my dear wife was mortified. But that setting raised the music to a higher level, and brought a keener awareness of the piece to the listener who was also a worshipper. For the 'performance' of the Requiem, if one can describe it in this way, transcended the customary production one would hear on a stage with orchestra and choir.

In St. Stephen's the orchestra was associated with the cathedral, whose choir led the singing, and whose clergy spoke the narrative. In contrast to the orchestral stage production with which we are accustomed, this was essentially an act of worship. Imagine the thrill of worship when a gathered congregation heard a new and original piece of sacred music by Mozart played during their own service of worship.

We cannot have a Bach to lead our choir or a Mozart to play our organ, or a Beethoven to compose new anthems for the choir. But we can experience the thrill of worship. The sense of anticipation electrified by these four dynamic words, "LET US WORSHIP GOD". Many acts of worship commence with what I consider a rather lifeless 'Good Morning, nice to see you' introduction. What alternative words can surpass the collective Call to Worship, 'Let us Worship God', and the comprehensive bending of the will under the authority of the Word of God signalled by the entry of the Bible? The encouragement of heart and soul in knowing that the days we have spent and the experiences we have known are themselves gathered into this act of worship, into this divine fellowship we enjoy with God in Jesus. The sense of personal re-assurance that our individual prayers are gathered into the collective prayers of a congregation. While these congregational prayers are themselves assumed into the perpetual prayers of Christ our Intercessor. This is the wonder of worship. The traditional Scottish Paraphrase captures the moment.

'Where high the heavenly temple stands,
The house of God not made with hands
Our great High Priest our nature wears,
The Guardian of mankind appears'

Some time ago I spent a Sunday morning in an entirely different way. Instead of conducting an act of worship I stood on the touchline of one among many football pitches. The matches were physically robust but played with thought and intelligence. The young players had obviously trained hard and prepared their tactics. They put everything into that game because it was possible that a scout from a senior football team might be watching. They were playing for the chance to make a name for themselves in professional football. They were playing for their future.

I thought to myself, 'What does our traditional Sunday service hold to compete with their vision for their future life, and to attract them into the pews of church and chapel'? With the diminishing congregations and declining attendances at worship there is a challenge for every church and chapel to create modern and attractive forms of worship. Perhaps churchgoers are too settled in their ways and habits, not always the right way nor a good habit. Perhaps we even take Jesus for granted. Does that hymn that thrilled many Boys' Brigade services still make you feel excited?

'We have an anchor that keeps the soul,
Steadfast and sure while the billows roll;
Fastened to the Rock which cannot move,
Grounded firm and deep in the Saviour's love'

The worship in the church never has been static, but with its own fluid movement has changed throughout the passing decades. Many complain that we are departing from the traditional hymns such as those composed by Charles Wesley.

Such an outlook fails to appreciate that Wesley's hymns were composed for the worship of ordinary people who could not sing the metrical psalms. Because of their novelty Wesley's hymns were banned from the established church. The same hostility greeted the introduction of the Scottish paraphrases. When the minister had the temerity to announce the singing of the new paraphrase the dissenters in the congregations snapped their books closed to register their disapproval. But modernisation in worship is taking place in the contemporary church scene. Creative worship, fresh hymns often using traditional melodies, an engagement with every generation through all-age worship, are offering in worship a Christian vision of life. And we are attracting the generation of young people who play football on a Sunday morning. This is the wonder of worship.

Just a Thought

He was a tradesman who still went to church **(Luke 4.16).** *His friends often worked night shift* **(Luke 5.5).** *One Sunday he helped a farmer rescue his trapped sheep* **(Matthew 12.11).** *Often he was a doctor called out on a Sunday to treat the sick* **(Matthew 12.9-14).** *He made time before he started work to be with God* **(Mark 1.35-39).** *He was never too tired before he went to bed for his evening devotion (***Matthew 14.23).** *Here was a man who knew the wonder of worship.*

He was called JESUS.

5 WORSHIP'S UNIVERSAL LANGUAGE

On another trip, this time to Krakow we visited the Basilica of St. Mary with its famous Veit Stoss Altar. This is the largest Altar of its kind and was created in 1477-1489. When the wings of the cabinet are closed twelve scenes from Mary's suffering are depicted. The artists who painted these original scenes used the poor people of Krakow as models, many of whom suffered terrible illnesses. But the paintings are so accurately executed that doctors today can diagnose their illnesses.

On the Sunday we attended a church service in the Basilica. The church was packed with ordinary people, especially young parents with their children. I could not follow the Order of Service, nor could I understand the Polish language. But this live act of worship, with that wondrous Altar Piece as a backdrop communicated its own language of praise and adoration to Almighty God. Anyone could have understood, grasped the meaning, and followed the progress of this act of worship. The scene in that Basilica created a divine dimension in which pure praise and human adoration were released. This service spoke the universal language of worship. The word 'adoration' perfectly describes the universal approach to God in worship. 'Ad' is the Latin word meaning 'towards', while 'oration' comes from the Latin word 'orare' to pray. In adoration we come to God through prayer, there is no way more fitting.

Everyone, irrespective of the language they speak or the religious tradition to which they belong, can approach God in the universal movement of adoration and worship. At the Reformation, when Martin Luther gave to the German people a Bible written in their native language and hymns they could sing, he released the power of worship into the lives of ordinary people. Luther helped to make worship the embracing experience in which all could participate. The same can be said about John Knox and the Scottish reformers. They wanted to take the Christian gospel into every part of Scotland, put the Bible into everyone's hand, and its message into every language.

For Christianity can be spoken and understood in every language, planted in every life, and discovered in the broad panorama of life.

Just a Thought
The Basilica of St. Mary in Krakow's main square has two twin towers. But one is larger and taller than the other. The towers were built by two brothers. When he saw that his brother's tower was superior to his, the first brother killed him. He then completed his own which was larger, but inferior, to the smaller one. The smaller tower belongs to the church, the larger one to the state. The city of Krakow with its majestic Basilica did not suffer much damage during the war. But what did that church see and hear? It overlooked the Kazimierz district in Krakow where the Jewish population had settled, confined in their ghetto. Did that church hear from their synagogue the Jewish praise to Jehovah and the reciting of the Shema, from worshippers as pious as its own? Did the owner of that factory where many Jews found sanctuary as well as work ever walk through the Basilica doors? (Oscar Schindler's factory was situated in the Jewish quarter). Did that church hear the tread of the death trains on their way to death camps? (Auschwitz and Birkenau are close to Krakow). In that Basilica the 'Ave Maria' was ever sung. But in these camps the 'Shema' of Israel and the 'Lord's Prayer 'of Christ were never silenced. Worship to God can be heard everywhere

6 WORSHIP-THE LANGUAGE OF THE SOUL

Worship is the language of the soul. When we worship we cannot pretend. We are seen in our true light by ourselves and by God who receives our worship. That is why the words of Beethoven's 'Missa Solemnis' are so apt and powerful. Many of these great Masses in classical music were not necessarily composed by believers. However, Beethoven's prayers contained in his diaries clearly show that he was a firm believer, if not a conventional one. For if he created his own monumental music in his voluminous compositions, then equally his belief was uniquely his own. Then the text of the 'Gloria' in the 'Missa Solemnis' vibrates with a personal passion

'We praise Thee, we bless Thee,
we worship Thee, we adore Thee'

Beethoven nurtured a very private religion, and this feature becomes immediately clear from the opening bars of the 'Missa Solemnis'. But this music was composed in a broken heart. Not only did Beethoven suffer from distressing domestic problems and from the fierce comments of his critics. But what is more he composed his music in the world of silence, for he became totally deaf. His music was his worship as we hear so clearly in the 'Pastoral', his 6th symphony. His praise was the language of the soul, a saddened and wounded soul.

So, in our worship we 'adore' God, that is we draw near to God through prayer and praise. Public worship can capture that authentic thrill, and declare a fundamental conviction that can find expression only in praise and worship to Almighty God. For the soul that declares 'Credo in unum Deum', 'I believe in one God' will want to express that belief by saying 'Adoro Te, propter magnam gloriam Tua', 'I adore Thee because of Thy great glory'. For the voice of public worship is the chorus of every worshipper. The prayers in public worship gather the prayers of every believer. The worship from every individual is not lost in the congregation's crowd but rather finds its true place in the environment of collective praise. All because worship is the language of the soul.

Just a Thought

Communion Sunday in a Presbyterian Kirk is a time of high occasion with the dressed pews, the Communion Table, the elders serving the people. Likewise in the chapel during the celebration of Mass there is an expectancy at the Preparation of the Altar and the Gifts. But often minister and priest will celebrate Communion in quieter places, the minister with an elderly soul unable to attend public worship and the priest with the dying. Then the soul is free to worship God in a way yet more tender and immediate. At many sick beds and in countless fireside scenes an altar of sacramental worship is often raised.

7 MEETING JESUS

The wonder of worship, its divine dimension and personal nature, these are but a few of the multi-faceted aspects of worship. There is another, there is the personal presence of Jesus Christ our Lord and Saviour. Bellini's great masterpiece painting of the 'Baptism of Christ' hangs in the church of the Sacred Cross, a very modest and unassuming church in Vicenza in northern Italy. From the moment I saw it I was captivated. Bellini (1431-1516) the 15th century master artist of Venice, used a canvas unique to this maritime centre. In addition these great painters were required to make their own paints. Bellini's mastery at using the Venice canvas and paint together with his consummate skills are readily seen in this particular painting.

While the contemporary Florentine painters relied on drawing and design, Bellini gave new prominence to colour. It was only natural that this should be so. The play of light in the lagoons around Venice irresistibly attracted this master painter. By his use of colours Bellini adds a richness to his paintings, and makes his figures very warm and human. Bellini's genius is so evident in 'The Baptism of Christ'. The robes of the attendant figures are in rich gold, blue and crimson while the robes of John the Baptist, though darker, also show this richness of colour. The central figure is Christ Jesus being baptised. He wears a simple loincloth, so light in colour that it shimmers between gold and pink. The next time Jesus would be robed with a loincloth would be at his crucifixion death on the cross, when his baptism would be completed. The painting is awesome. One can study it clearly with the aid of artificial light, when the rich colours flood our view. Or again, I studied it without the artificial light in the darker but more natural shade of the church. But under both conditions the picture reaches out to embrace the beholder. The eyes of Jesus Christ the central figure seem to gaze steadfastly into the destiny set before him by his baptism. But at the same time these steadfast eyes seem to follow the beholder wherever one stands in the church. Imagine the thrill of worshipping in that church of the Sacred Cross with that masterpiece hanging on the church wall, with the eyes of Jesus ever upon the worshipper.

How much greater the thrill of public worship in every church, chapel and meeting place when it is not a painting of Jesus that is seen but the living presence of Jesus who is felt. In the final analysis our worship is our meeting with Jesus. Very often our great cathedrals were built in the shape of the cross. But always and in every occasion our worship is cross-shaped. Worship is a dialogue between the Saviour and the saved, His the word of grace, ours the language of gratitude. For only the gratitude of the saved can answer the grace of the Saviour. We worship our God and Father under the cross of Christ. We are led to this meeting place called worship by the magnetism of the Spirit.

To this meeting place we come from our side, our temporal scene, our human faith, our yearnings and aspirations as well as our failures and regrets. But to this same meeting place Christ comes from his divine dimension. Into our broken prayers he pours fullness of meaning. Under our explanations for errors he places his hands of understanding. Into that hurt he pours the oil of healing. For our fear he gathers us in embracing arms, the fear is still there, but now we will confront it. Then we know that in the Spirit God is with us in his Son. Worship is that sublime moment when we reach out to touch and be touched by God whom we encounter when we meet with Jesus. At that moment our time is finger tipped with eternity. That is what it is like to be with Jesus in worship. In the 2nd movement in Beethoven's 9th Violin Sonata, the 'Kreutzer', one moment electrifies the listener. The accompanying piano enters as it were into a dialogue with the major violin instrument. This conversation between violin and piano continues for many bars and then concludes in a moment of pure silence. How much greater when in worship we hold dialogue with Jesus.

Just a Thought

'To meet with you without space
To be with you but in no place
To hear you wordlessly speaking
To embrace and be embraced by you without touch
To hold salvation, faith our only token
To walk by grace and not by sight
To meet with you and find our God
Jesus, this is how we worship you, with the Father in the Spirit'

8   THE SACRED MAJESTY OF THE WORD OF GOD

John Calvin (1509-1564) has helped every Christian to understand better the Christian faith. In the intervening centuries his name became synonymous with a rigid theology called 'calvinism'. Nowadays, Calvin's writings are grossly neglected. But Calvin was more than an intellectual theologian. He was primarily a pastor and his teaching was directed to his congregation in Geneva. In one of his commentaries he wrote, 'How great a thing it is that in teaching the oracles of God they (preachers) are representatives of Christ. So much carelessness (in preaching) comes from the fact that the sacred majesty of the Word of God is only kept in mind by a few' **("Commentary 1st Peter 4.11")**

'The sacred majesty of the Word of God'. What a wonderful way to describe the Gospel and the teaching of the Bible. The story is told of Sir Walter Scott, that on his deathbed he asked his manservant to 'Hand me down the 'Big Book', the Bible. Today the teachings of the Bible are disregarded, and its authority disobeyed. Lack of knowledge about the Bible is universal and pervasive. For that matter do Christians know their Bible as they ought? Today let us exult in the magnificence of the Bible, in the sacred majesty of the Word of God.

The church's preacher and teacher must first discover the sacred majesty of the Word of God upon whose truth all teaching and preaching will be founded. For there can be no true preaching until the preacher first sees and reveres the sacred majesty of the Word. Then in speaking the preacher will assist the members of the congregation to discover for themselves the sacred majesty of the Word of God. Finally, both preacher and congregation will together stand in wonder at the holy beauty of the Word of God, and bow in obedience beneath its living truth. This is the majestic Word of God, the foundation of our Christian teaching.. The Gospel of St. John has an assured place in world literature. John Calvin described John's Gospel in this way. He wrote that the first three Gospels show us Jesus' outward life, what he said and did. But John's Gospel reveals Jesus' heart and soul', his inner self. John chapter 6 forms a continuous narrative covering two days of teaching. Jesus told the people that He was their Saviour and Redeemer. Many people and not a few disciples deserted Jesus. Jesus then asked the inner Twelve if they wanted to leave. Peter replied for them all *'Lord to whom can we go, you have the words of eternal life'* **(John 6.68).**

Has contemporary society completely forgotten Jesus' teaching, and totally disregarded the fact that the words of our Lord Jesus are the words of eternal life? Do we in church and chapel stand guilty of the same offence? Jesus taught the people then, and still speaks to us today, with words mighty and powerful. *'The people were astonished at Jesus' teaching, for Jesus taught with authority'* **(Matthew 7.28-29).** But the same Jesus whose words were the very authority and wisdom of God the Father, died on the cross for the forgiveness of the world's sin and the salvation of the world's soul. So, if the words of Jesus the Teacher are powerful with God's authority, then the words of Jesus the Saviour are saving unto life.

When Jesus spoke mighty things happened. Jesus uttered life-restoring words to a child, *'Talitha cumi, little child arise'* **(Mark 5.41).** Jesus gave strong moral words to the poor woman, words of forgiveness and salvation, *'Go and sin no more'* **(John 8.11).** Jesus pronounced pure and holy words against evil and darkness, *'Be silent and come out from this man'* **(Mark 1.25).** *'Father forgive them, they know not what they do'* **(Luke 23.34).** Jesus the Saviour spoke these eternal words on the cross. They will always remain saving words for the believing soul. That is why the words of the Bible treasure the 'sacred majesty of the Word of God'.

'God so loved the world that he gave us his only begotten Son that whosoever believeth in him, should not perish but have everlasting life' **(John 3.16).**

Just a Thought

'In the beginning was the Word, and the Word was with God and the Word was God. The Word was in the beginning with God. The Word became flesh and dwelt among us full of grace and truth' **(John 1. 1 & 14)**

9 WORSHIP – A LOST WORLD

When the Spanish conquistadors sailed across the Atlantic ocean to discover and invade South America one danger always threatened. The shortage of fresh drinking water cost many brave lives. The story is told of one expedition that successfully crossed the Atlantic ocean and started to sail up the Amazon river. At its mouth the Amazon is so wide that its riverbanks cannot be seen. The sailors imagined they were still at sea, while in reality they were sailing in a river of fresh water. With men dying by the hour they had only to lower their buckets into the river to tap a source of fresh drinking water. The same is true for worship in the church. If only men and women realised there is a church or chapel round the corner. It is filled by decent people like themselves. It offers an hour of peace and gentleness. It guarantees a chance to draw breath and recharge the batteries. But its greatest attraction is its opportunity to meet with Jesus.

When I came out of college I knew plenty book-taught theology. But when I served my probationer year in the south side of Glasgow I saw Christianity in real life. Men exposed to the heat and danger of a blast furnace, men and women working on an uncompromising production line where target figures counted for everything. Yet they always attended their church. My first charge was in a fishing community in the Highlands. These fishermen were brave sailors, taking small boats out to sea in all weathers. But their boats remained in harbour over the weekend and they attended their church without fail. These fishermen and heavy industry workers found something of God in their worship. That 'something of God' is still there for the community at large.

'What life have you if you have not life together?
There is no life that is not in community,
And no community not lived in praise of God'
(T.S. Eliot. 'The Rock' 1934)

If the message in T S Eliot's poetry was appropriate seventy years ago, it is far more relevant in our contemporary society. The British nation is historically associated with the Christian religion represented by the Church. But nowadays the fabric in which Christian faith and worship are interwoven into British society has been torn asunder. We are no longer a Christian nation, believing and worshipping according to Christianity. This raises two fundamental questions. First, what happens when a society ceases to worship God? Second, why have our Christian faith and practices become so unattractive?

What happens when a society ceases to worship God? To help us in our study we enter the world of the Old Testament, to listen to the prophetic voice of these great figures. The Jewish people divide the Old Testament, their Hebrew Bible, into three sections, the Law, the Prophets, and the (holy) Writings. The Law of Moses found within the first five books of the Bible, and the teachings of the Prophets are the twin pillars upon which Judaism is founded. Moses represents the Law, and Elijah the Prophets. So, when Christ was transformed on the Mount of Transfiguration the three disciples saw Moses and Elijah talking with the Lord **(Matthew 17.1-8).** Jesus continues and fulfils Israel's historic witness to God. When a nation or society turns its back on Jesus then it rejects the guidance and care of God

A yawning chasm is opening between church and society. The widespread neglect of things Christian is clearly evident in many ways, the lack of knowledge concerning the message of the Bible, the awkward way people enter the setting of church or chapel for a wedding or a funeral, unfamiliar as they are through years of absence and the universal abandonment of everything associated with Christianity. There appears to be an ever-increasing chasm between our contemporary society and the Christian faith. Has society gone too far, has the divide between secular society and Christianity become unbridgeable? Many claim they do not need to rely on God, and that they enjoy a very full and successful life without the need for any faith. Others claim they do not see any relevance in the rites and customs of church worship. Has the world of worship been lost? A Boys' Brigade captain took his Company section into the actual church to prepare for a forthcoming church service. The boys in the Company were drawn from the local congregation and from the surrounding parish. But instead of running through the Order of Service with the boys, the captain found himself explaining to the boys what were the various items in the church, such as the Communion Table, the Baptismal font, the pulpit and lectern.

However such thoughts barely touch the central issue. What place does worship fill in the human mind and consciousness? Worship is born in our sense of wonder at our place as human beings within the Universe. This sense of wonder, leading to worship, is as strong as our instinct for survival. This elemental dimension of worship is brilliantly expressed in Psalm 8.

'When I look to the heavens, the work of your fingers,
the moon and the stars which you have established
who are people that you are mindful of us
You have made people a little less than God
And crowned us with glory and honour'
(Psalm   8.3-5)

The Hebrew name for God is the 'living One'. God told Moses **(Exodus 3.13-14)** 'I am the living God' That is the ultimate reason why worship is vitally essential for every human being. Worship takes a person into the dimension of life and God. But in a personal way, worship gives true meaning to the life of every individual. That is why worship is so fundamental, and its absence so crippling, to the human mind and conscience. Remember the beginning of the Ten Commandments *'I am the Lord your God'* **(Exodus 20.2)**? The Large Haldron Collider at CERN in Switzerland may highlight new dimensions in human experience and knowledge. But it does not require a 17 mile long collider with protons travelling at nearly the speed of light in order to discover the divine dimension. A person need only open his life to Jesus. Our God and Father who meets us in Jesus is still waiting *'I said, here am I, here am I, to a nation that did not call on my name I spread out my hands all day to a rebellious people who walk in a way that is not good'* **(Isaiah 65 2).**

A Prayer

Eternal God
    'Open closed eyes that everyone will see that you are here
        Break down the resistance that pretends you do not matter
    Engage with the serious soul who doubts
        and in that doubting cannot believe
    Encourage that mind that has seen too much
        and in its seeing can no longer trust human nature
           and wonders about trusting God
    Listen to the believer's worship
        broken words, unspoken prayers, unfinished hymns
    For praise broken sacramentally is God-blessed
        Affirm the one who denies you
    Remember the one who forgets you
        Study in the researcher's world
           even when his findings leave to you no room
    Attend the obedient soldier now wounded
        a broken body, 'This is my body broken for you'
In Christ
    Visit the unlikely places where no one expects to find you
        Be health to the addict to make him sane
    Walk the streets of the homeless to lead them home
        Speak to the prisoner in that cell
           with no steel bars between you
               because you are locked in that cell with him
    You are both patient and doctor in that ward
        in the diseased body and the trained mind
In all places and at all times be God, be yourself
    Then likewise in everything we can be ourselves
Be our God, braver than we can ever imagine
    in your Courageous Christ
        make us courageous
Bring Jesus close to us all

Eternal God
> May Jesus come quickly
> Then we shall see the sacred majesty
>> of Jesus the living Word of God
> AMEN

One Word in Conclusion

This is the prayer of Solomon at the dedication of his temple. It is the expression of all worship

'But will God indeed dwell with man on the earth?
Heaven and highest heaven cannot contain God
O Lord my God. hearken to the cry and prayers that
your servant prays before you, that your eyes may
be open day and night towards this place where
you have set your name. Listen to the prayers of your
servants, and when you hear, forgive'
(2 Chronicles 6.18-21)

Chapter 2

THE THINGS WE ADD

In his closing speech at the Nurenberg War Trials in 1946, Sir Hartley Shawcross, Britain's Chief Prosecutor read from a German eyewitness account of a mass execution of Jews in the Baltic.

'Without screaming or weeping these people undressed and stood around in family groups, kissed each other and said farewells. During the fifteen minutes I stood nearby I heard no pleas for mercy. I watched a family of about eight people, a man and a woman with their two daughters, their children and their old mother. The old woman with white hair was holding the child in her arms, and tickling it; the baby cooed with delight. The couple looked on with tears. The father was holding the hand of a ten-year old boy, speaking to him softly as the boy fought his tears. The father pointed to the sky and seemed to explain something to him. Then they moved into the pit in front of the SS man with the machine gun. I heard a series of shots'.

That scene is so deeply moving, and so comprehensively instructive. Three generations in that close family circle retained affection and beauty when confronted by stark cruelty. They retained such a degree of dignity that they would not ask for help. With only fifteen minutes of life remaining they were still able to share kindness, laughter and love. They affirmed the fullness of life at the very moment when their own lives were to be savagely ended. They added so much of life to that scene of death.

We are given the gift of one life. But what we do with that life will remain the overriding consideration. Perhaps this is the deepest meaning in Jesus' parable. **(Matthew 25.14-28).**

1   THE THINGS WE ADD – OUR TEARS

A little tale. A junior angel watched the creator God at work in his world. After God created everything in the world, God made two people, one a man, the other a woman. The little angel was fascinated by this perfect creation. For he realised that the man and woman had minds to think, hearts to love, and souls to worship God. 'God, you are a genius, they are perfect', he exclaimed. 'But why did you put these tears in their eyes and upon their cheeks?' The creator God, accustomed as He was to such praise, seemed slightly embarrassed. 'Little angel', God replied, 'I did not put these tears into their eyes, that they would run down their cheeks'. 'They themselves put them there'.

Everyone has been given one life, with hands to work, heads to think and hearts to love. But what we do with our life is so important How do we employ or neglect our talents? The changes we make, the things we add, how we use or misuse our bodies. Let us think of the things we add to our life. We remember that we put tears into our eyes.

'Jesus wept' **(John 11.35)**, the shortest verse in the whole Bible, yet it speaks volumes. Jesus was very fond of this family, the two sisters and their brother **(John 11.5).** Perhaps their home provided a welcome retreat for our Lord. There was something final in that scene when our Lord came to the grave of his friend **(John 11.1-16).** We too have often found ourselves there. Then our tears are our only words. But the tears in our eyes are the words from our hearts

Do not be reluctant to cry. The good Lord was being good to us when he gave us the ability to shed tears. When we try to fill an empty life, and comfort a broken heart our words sound futile. 'I'm sorry' says so little, so badly. But when that broken friend sees through tear-filled eyes your distress, and hears in silence the message of the heart translated by your tears, then you are standing at that Bethany grave where 'Jesus wept'.

'O Jerusalem, Jerusalem, how I would have gathered your children as a hen gathers her brood. But you would not' **(Matthew 23.37).** Jesus wept tears over the city, willing and yearning that the people would return to God and receive from God the good news of salvation. How final are Christ's words, 'But you would not'. Often our tears plead for something to change. The doctor's report confirming what we suspected. Our sense of failure when our wholesome advice is rejected. The three teenagers were wild but never vicious. But one night their pranks escalated into crime. They were caught, charged, and later appeared before the sheriff in private. That was the procedure before the introduction of the Children's Hearing system. Two of the boys left the court with careless indifference. But, ashen faced the third blurted out, 'Now I have a police record'. Something of lasting significance had changed in his life. At the other extreme, the tears of joy at the birth of a child will be the infant's baptism by human love.

The tears we add to our life. There is another New Testament scene where we feel hot and bitter tears. After the wonder of the Last Supper in the Upper Room, the disciples had gone to the Garden of Gethsemane. There the riotous crowd led by Judas had captured Jesus and taken him to the high priest. The night air gripped him and Peter edged closer to the fire. But he was recognised by the temple maid, *'You also were with Jesus of Nazareth'* and by the other bystanders. *'You are one of them, your accent betrays you'* **(Matthew 26.69-73).** With curses Peter denied all knowledge of Jesus. And we read, *'Peter went out and wept bitterly'* **(Matthew 26.75).** Sometimes we shed hot and bitter tears. Tears of regret for something that will never be undone. Tears of loss for that loved one meant more to us than life itself. Tears of resignation for we know nothing will change. The heart of the woman who washed Christ feet with her tears and dried them with her hair was sore oppressed **(Luke 7. 36-38).** Like Peter, we cradle tears in our eyes, when we walked through the darkness of the night. There are many events in our life, and how we wish we could change them, even obliterate them, as if they had not happened. If that memory hidden in the past still disturbs then remember the deep and comforting verse from the Bible, *'If your heart condemns you, God is greater than your heart, and he knows (and understands) everything'* **(1 John 3.20).**

'Jesus prayed the more earnestly, and his sweat became like great drops of blood' **(Luke 22.44).** Christ cried bitterly in the Garden of Gethsemane. Christ still cries with the same eternal passion for his children. Now if we love Christ, and shed our tears in faith and compassion for one another, then Christ will make our tears to become like his. Christ will use our tears to heal and save. Our tears will be part of Christ's saving work. Tears are created in our heart, they flow from our eyes But Jesus will re-direct their flow to wash away someone's sorrow, and refresh another's tired soul

Gerald Manley Hopkins once wrote,
'Christ was himself but one and lived and died but once
But the Holy Spirit makes of every Christian another Christ
(Christ) lives a million lives in every age'

A Meditation

'The Lord God had yet to cause the rain to fall upon the earth', but a mist went up from the ground and watered the face of the earth'
(Genesis 2.5-6)

Creator God
But when that rain did come
    was each rain droplet the tears of God's joy
      to see the earth that it was good?
    And was that mist the gentle vapour of God's breath
      as God inspired life into all things.
'And the rain fell upon the earth these forty days and nights'
    (Genesis 7.12).

Creator God
    Were these rains but the flood of God's tears, bitter tears?
      'The Lord was sorry he had made man on the earth'
      (Genesis 6.6).
        the first tears to wash away man's errors
          next, tears to plead to his darkened mind and soul
            then, from God's broken heart, tears to cleanse
            a lovely earth.

Healing God

> May Jesus use us and let our tears flow for the healing of a
> wounded soul
>> the baptism of healing
>>> the droplet of cleansing

Gentle God

> *Your Son did weep, 'Jesus wept'* **(John 11.35).**

But Christ's sorrow was translated into sympathy – by tears.

> may Jesus use us allowing our tears to flow
>> for the healing of a wounded soul
>>> droplets of cleansing
>>>> a baptism of healing with tears

Saving God

> 'Were you there when they crucified my Lord?'

My Lord but your Son

> How greatly did you weep at Calvary?

The Father's tears more painful in a heart eternally pure

> God's tears infinitely enduring, unrestrained by time and
> space

God grieving and yearning, seeking and saving

> How greatly did you weep at Calvary?

'God shall wipe away all tears from their eyes' **(Revelation 7.17).**

> *'They took the body of Jesus and laid it in a tomb'*
> **(John 19. 38-42).**

Gentle God, did you wipe away all tears from His eyes, the
Broken One?

> One day, will you wipe away all tears from our eyes?

AMEN

2   THE SHAPE OF COMPASSION

We are thinking about the things we add to life, and how we use our talents and qualities. We put tears into our eyes. We can also create kindness with our deeds, and express sympathy with our words, because we nurse compassion in our heart.

Elsa Brandstrom was the daughter of the Swedish ambassador to Russia during the 1st World War. She saw the wretched plight of the German prisoners being transported to Siberia.   What she saw changed her life. She became a nurse and started to visit the prison camps. She became the Angel of Siberia for them because she surrendered her privileged life in order to help these prisoners. She fought the brutality of the prison guards and she fell under the suspicion of the authorities. She witnessed unspeakable horror and unrelieved suffering. After the war she worked tirelessly to help the orphaned children of both German and Russian soldiers killed in battle. She herself was imprisoned and this treatment broke her health. At the outbreak of the 2nd World War she was forced to emigrate from Germany to America, where during the war years she helped European refugees. She shaped her life with compassion. (This lovely story can be found in Paul Tillich's volume of sermons 'The New Being').

The story of Christ healing the leper **(Mark 1.40-45)** clearly reveals the dimensions of Christ's compassion. The leper approaches Jesus, *'If you will you can heal me'*. We read, *'Jesus was moved with compassion'* **(Mark 1.41)**. But the Greek word for 'compassion' is virtually untranslatable. It is one of the strongest words in the New Testament. It tells us that Jesus was moved to the very depth of his being by the man's illness. Jesus was deeply upset by indignation coupled with infinite compassion. Jesus was not simply 'sorry' for the man. Jesus was profoundly moved.

This story happened to me when I was a teenager. I was brought up in country villages where my father was the local policeman. I often saw a family in grief, their lives shattered by their loss, an accident, or a bereavement Yet, welling up from their grief, family members shared their enormous compassion for one another. This gives us some indication of Jesus' compassion. Jesus then touched the man, thereby making himself ceremonially unclean. But he touched the man with the pure and sovereign power of God to heal, cleanse and save. As one commentator wrote, *'The ceremonial law gives place to the law of love when the two come into collision'* **(H van der Loos 'The Miracles of Jesus')**.

Often we must be sufficiently brave to share our concern with others, and to accept with undefended feelings their burdens. Our approach may be misunderstood, our motives questioned, our offer of help rejected. But often it is only such a courageous gesture that can break into the isolation of another's grief. Often it is only our brave initiative that will bring down the barriers of fear and suspicion, thus enabling another person to be comforted by love and understanding. If we open our heart in concern then we expose ourselves to hurt and distress. But we should be brave. For a sorrow shared is a sorrow halved. Comfort shared is comfort increased. Jesus showed no hesitation in embracing the pitiful leper. We must show considerable courage to feel for others in a similar way.

This picture of Christ's infinite compassion embracing the leper colours other events in our Lord's ministry. At the conclusion of the eleven narratives showing Christ among the people **(Matthew 8-9)** Matthew wrote, *'Jesus was moved with compassion at the sight of the people. They were like sheep without a shepherd'* **(Matthew 9.36).**

When Jesus saw the widow of Nain burying her only son, we read that Jesus showed infinite compassion for her **(Luke 7.13).** The Good Samaritan was terribly upset when he saw the plight of the man attacked by thieves **(Luke 10.33).** Likewise, the old father, when he saw his returning prodigal son, was moved to compassion **(Luke 15. 20).** In all these instances, whether it is parable stories or real life incidents, this same strong Greek word for 'compassion' is employed. Christ's was the infinite compassion of God embracing every human situation.

Another narrative shows the irrepressible feelings created when two compassionate souls meet. The father of the epileptic boy came to Jesus, *'If you can do anything, help us, have compassion on us'* **(Mark 9. 14-29 especially. v22).** The father's feelings for his son are palpable. We are hurt by the father's distress. We feel for the plight of the boy. We see seeking eyes focussed on Jesus, the outstretched hands of a father at his wits end. *'Help us with your compassion'.*

'Lord I believe, help thou my unbelief'. How often have we echoed that cry? When two particles of atomic material collide there is an atomic explosion. When two compassionate souls come together a new world of mercy is created

When two masses of gas and dust collide in the deep reaches of outer space a new star is often born. When Jesus met that father and

41

his boy a new life experience was created, like the birth of a star. Christ's compassion to heal met the father's yearning for relief. The urge to provide help enfolded the experience of weakness. The movement to heal fused with the need for wholeness and renewal. The infinite compassion of the Saviour Christ met the total compassion of the suffering father. Did Christ see in the figure of that suffering father something of the pure and infinite suffering of his God and Father for his children? That day divine and human passion fused as one. The day was soon to come when God's compassion and humanity's need would be fused forever on the Cross. Simone Weil once wrote,

> 'God wears himself out through the infinite thickness of time and space in order to reach the soul.
> The soul, starting from the opposite end,
> makes the same journey that God makes towards it.
> And that is the cross'.

Let us resolve to deepen our feelings for one another. Let us be strong enough to carry one another's burdens. May we be brave enough to feel another's pain, and grieve with that broken heart. '*Put on then, as God's holy ones, compassion, kindness, lowliness, meekness and patience'* **(Colossians 3.12).**

Postscript.

(Mark 9.14-29) That evening their little house was peaceful. The young father, still overwhelmed by the events of the day, watched his little boy, now healed, move freely through the room. He knocked into a chair, but father and mother did not jump as before, fearing another seizure. 'Can I blow out the candle light?' he asked. They looked at each other. They had always feared that in his attacks their little boy would knock over the lamp stand with its naked flame and cause a fire. ''Yes you can', said a loving mother.

A Prayer

Gentle God, we seek to pray for children
> '*Suffer the little children to come unto me and forbid them not For of such is the kingdom of heaven'* **(Matthew 19.14).**
Heavenly Father,
> We remember how the heart of Jesus cared for the children

Even as the eternal soul of God yearns for men and
women, his children
We call you Father, only because you treat us as your children.
'Like as a father pities his children
So the Lord has pity upon them that honour him'
(Psalm 103.13).
So we pray, strong Father
Guard your children
From the evil that molests a child, destroying innocence and
body
From the cruel war that makes a child an orphan
From the evil thinking that justifies the starving of children
Unforgivable thinking, on the very border beyond God's
mercy
'Whoever receives a child in my name receives me.
But whoever causes one of these little ones to suffer,
It would be better for him ....' **(Matthew 18.5-6).**
Gentle God
Your Son spoke life-giving words to a child
'Talitha Cumi' 'Little child arise' **(Mark 5.41)**
We pray for those who care for children
Nurses and doctors in hospitals
Carers helping a sick child nearing the end of a life
that has only just begun
Parents in their homes and family circles
Gentle God
Your Son brought peace to a distraught father and his little
boy
'Lord I believe, help me in my unbelief' **(Mark 9.24)**
There once was a child who went with her mother into a
chamber,
and was gassed
But she left behind a shoe to remind us
she had walked across God's land
and a doll to tell us she had been happy.
When we no longer walk across God's land
We will gladly leave our little world to our children
AMEN

3 LIFE-CHANGING QUALITIES

The qualities we possess if used properly can change lives. When Primo Levi was imprisoned at Auschwitz he was helped by a fellow Italian called Lorenzo, who was a civilian prison worker. For six months Lorenzo gave Primo extra food, provided him with clothing, and wrote a postcard to his family in Italy. But by his manner, as much as the extra food, he constantly reminded Primo that there was a world of goodness outside the camp, a world worth striving for. Lorenzo displayed human qualities and encouraged Primo Levi to remember that he himself was a human being. Lorenzo changed and saved Primo Levi.

Jesus told the parable of the master who entrusted his affairs to his servants. He gave to each respectively five, two, and one talent **(Matthew 25.14-25).** The word 'talent' is unique. Firstly in the New Testament the word only appears in this section of Matthew's Gospel. Secondly it has a two-fold meaning. Older people will remember shopping when goods were weighed on the old fashioned scales. On one side the bag of sugar was positioned. But on the other arm of the scales the 1lb weight was placed. When the two arms of the scales stood equal then the correct amount of the merchandise had been measured. Now the Greek word for talent is 'talanton'. It means both the merchandise being bought and the weight by which it was measured. The word 'talent' then passed from the goods in the market place to the moral and religious qualities possessed by an individual. But its two-fold meaning was retained. So a 'talent' in the New Testament refers to a person's ability, and the importance placed upon that ability by God. In our Christian life the word talent means Jesus' gift to us, and the value Jesus places upon it.

Paul's letter to the 'Ephesians' is called the Queen of the Letters' because it contains so many wonderful thoughts. Paul outlines the gifts given to his followers by Jesus

'His (Christ) gifts were that some would be apostles, some prophets, some evangelists, some pastors and teachers' **(Ephesians 4.11).**

Before Jesus left us at the ascension our resurrected Lord gave his gifts, his talents, to his believers, just as the absent master in the parable committed his possessions to his servants for proper use.

But Christ's gift to us is like the talent in the parable. It is a gift, but Jesus places his own value and importance on it. The Christian talents we possess are not optional extras. They are strategically important to Christ. Our abilities are necessary tools in Christ's Kingdom. These Christian gifts are cross-created qualities established to expand the Kingdom of God. Christ will want to know how we use our gifts. Are we like the servant with five talents whose efforts made a further five for his master? Or are we like the careless servant who buried his solitary talent?

Christ Jesus took me from the legal profession and directed me into the ministry. When I appear before the judgment seat on high the Lord will want to know how I used his talent. Christ has placed a strategic importance on his talent. Christ intends to fulfil certain objectives through its wise use. Christ will assess me on how I have used his gift The criterion is simple. Do we change people's lives in and with our Christian example and use of our talent? It can work. I know a lady who eliminated bad language in the office just by her presence. You leave your house every Sunday morning for church and chapel. You can never know what impression you are creating in some observing neighbour. Your attitude may just be the strong word or deed that is helping someone through a period of critical strain. Unconsciously you may be changing lives.

But, at the end of the day, do you realise that you are also helping Jesus? Jesus relies on his followers to speak his word and show his life. Our witness is vital to the Kingdom. God's Kingdom is founded on our Lord's Easter passion. We point to Jesus. For the cost of our talent was the price Jesus paid on the cross. At the end may we hear Jesus say, *'Well done, good and faithful servant'* **(Matthew 25.21).**

Reinhold Niebuhr and his brother Richard were two very influential theologians in America at the end of the 19th and the beginning of the 20th century. They focused on the involvement of Christian morality and principles in the rapidly developing American industries, such as the car factories in Detroit. These two brothers highlighted in their writings how the use of Christian qualities was essential to society at large.

A Prayer
Gentle God
May we use Christ's talent with hope, that it will aid and support the fallen
May we share Christ's gift in love, knowing the love of the heart strengthens the work of the hand
May we trust that the work we undertake for Christ will find a place in the structure of his kingdom.
AMEN

4   TRUE VALUES

This little article was originally written for Mothering Sunday. In former times the significance of Mothering Sunday was more personal than commercial. On this Sunday young girls in service were allowed home to their families. They brought a gift to their mothers. It was a 'Simnel Cake', similar in shape to a pork pie but filled with plum-pudding mixture. Mothering Sunday highlights family and home. These are some of life's 'true values'. Often only the bad stories about young people appear in the press. But there are thousands of young people leading wholesome young lives, creating for themselves purpose-filled careers. Young students who work to pay for university and college education. It is not easy for a young couple to buy a house, obtain and then finance a mortgage, and start their family. These young families face far greater challenges than we did at the beginning of our adult lives. They are our strength and hope for the future. They will safeguard the true value of family life in society.

Family life as we know it was created in the Christian community of the New Testament. In the Greek and Roman households the father of the house dominated the family. Minor children were virtually the possession of the father, while his wife was little more than a housebound child-bearer. It was Paul, the great champion of human values who liberated women and children. In his letter to 'Colossians' Paul wrote, *'Wives honour your husbands'*. But then he added, *'Husbands love and care for your wives'*. Nobody had ever imagined such a husband-wife relationship. Paul engineered a similar revolution in the relationship between parents and children. He wrote, *'Children obey your parents in everything'*. But then he balanced this teaching, *'Fathers do not provoke your children lest they be discouraged'.* Nobody had ever described the family in this wholesome way. **(See Colossians 3.18-25).**

It was in home and school where many children received their first teaching about Jesus and the Christian faith. John Baillie was one of three brothers who were theological giants in the 20th century Scottish church. They were brought up in a strict Calvinistic household in Gairloch where his father was the Free Church minister. He was taught the Catechisms sitting on his father's knee. He understood little of these early lessons. But his first awareness of God was awakened when he saw his strict father go down on his knees in prayer acknowledging someone greater than himself. Christianity, life's true value, is often first taught in the home.

In our church marriage service we declare that our society can be strong only where the marriage bond is revered and the family circle safeguarded. For the family is the building brick for the nation. At the end of the 2nd World War John Baillie chaired a nationwide committee which published a monumental report 'God's Will for Church and Nation'. This report was a rallying call to the British nation in the immediate aftermath of the war, and a source of encouragement for the whole nation. When the family unit is strong the nation will grow. When the family respects Christ the nation will obey Christ. By way of contrast the archbishop of Canterbury shook both church and nation with ill-considered remarks that threatened the foundation of Christianity and the stability of the law in this country. By the same token where the family church is strong and healthy the national Church will be a shining beacon for its generation. At present it is but a flickering candle in contemporary society. In a recent interview Archbishop Desmond Tutu predicted that a national church which failed to address the major global issues would be neglected by the public at large. The church must rediscover its identity and value as *'the body of Christ'* **(Ephesians 4. 1-6).** The established churches need to earn the respect of the public at large.

Let us re-discover the true worth of Christianity in Britain as a whole and in Scotland in particular. Scotland's rich Christian heritage is being lost through neglect. The Bible is being ignored and Christian teaching is simply unknown. Lives are being destroyed through alcohol and drug abuse. Violence through the blade culture is increasing. As soon as the moral restraints of our Christian faith are loosened then extreme behaviour is unleashed. As a nation we need to reach out for Christian faith's strong support. The New Testament teaches us proper moral behaviour, encourages higher standards, and brings God into our human experiences. These are the true values in life, and a society is ruined with their absence. When Britain as a whole, and within the UK Scotland as a nation, began to dismantle the fabric of Christianity within the nation, the political leaders and the British public began to dismantle the nation itself.

We are a nation ignorant about things Christian. The Lord's Prayer is unknown, the Beatitudes are not followed, and the laws of the Ten Commandments are forever being broken. The Bible is a closed book, encircled with the chain of ignorance, it cannot open its pages to a needy generation nor reveal its truth to an erring people. Is it a co-incidence that the levels of violence in this country have increased as the awareness of moral Christian teaching has decreased? A nation's true values are safeguarded by its families. May you be blessed in your family in every season of the year, and not only on a Mothering Sunday. *'I bow my knee unto God the Father by whose name every family in heaven and on earth is named (and blessed)* **(Ephesians 3.14-15)**

A Meditation

Gentle God,
The Teacher did say
> *'Be not anxious about your life, what you shall eat or drink'*
> **(Matthew 6.25).**
> But our heart loves the things we have rather than the person we are
> Have we still not learned that we do not live by bread alone?
> **(Matthew 4.4).**

The Teacher did say
> *'Seek ye first the kingdom of God and God's righteousness'*
> **(Matthew 6.33).**
> But God's kingdom unseen is a kingdom unloved

And to this day they still mock the Righteous One, and
crucify his goodness

The Teacher did say

> *'You are the salt of the earth, the light of the world, the city
> set on a hill;* **(Matthew 5.13-15)**

But if Christ finds the salt is tasteless,
> will Christ throw us away?

If the Light of the World looks in vain for reflections of his
radiance
> only to find gloom, for the darkness has dimmed the light
> **(John 1.5).**
> will he remove the lamp stand that has failed?
> **(Revelation 2.1).**

If Christ the Lord, the reigning Lord, looks for a righteous
nation
> like a city set on a hill, but finds instead only the ruins of
> righteousness
> will it not be better for Sodom and Gomorrah on that
> day? **(Matthew 10.15)**

Great God, we pray
> Teach us your ways, that our nation will say
> *'O house of Jacob, come let us walk in the light of the Lord'*
> **(Isaiah 2.5)**

Great God we pray
> Show us your way that this nation will turn to the Lord
> *'God has shown you, O man, what is good,*
> *and what does the Lord require of you*
> *but to do justice, to love kindness,*
> *and to walk humbly with your God'* **(Micah 6.8)**

5   OUR CROSS

> *'If anyone will come after me let him deny himself*
> *and take up his cross and follow me'* **(Mark 8.34)**

We are discovering the different ways to use our life, our talents and
abilities. The ultimate purpose to which we can devote our life lies in
bending our will to the way of God found in Jesus Christ. The way of

God leads us into a life of service but in that service we will find true and lasting freedom. This is not a mere contradiction, nor a simplistic play of words. For when we follow God in obedience and service then we discover we are journeying on God's way of eternal life. Like the psalmist we ask *'Lead me in the way everlasting'* **(Psalm 139.24)**. But, God's way of life can be hard to follow and few want to walk along its rough path. *'The way is hard that leads to life and those who find it are few'* **(Matthew 7.14)**. Often we are constrained to *'go the second mile'* **(Matthew 5.41)**. But often that second mile has no signpost to tell us we can stop and rest. Nobody measures the second mile. But we are guided by a set of footprints with red marks. Somebody with bruised and wounded feet walked this way before us.

The entrance to God's way of life in Jesus is very narrow. Many cannot find that entrance gate because it is so small. But many more are deterred by its shape, it is shaped like a cross. *'Enter by the narrow gate'* **(Matthew 7.13).**

Jesus tells us that for us his life will be the way of the cross. *'Follow me'* **(Mark 1.17).** The disciples remembered their first encounter with Jesus. They had felt a magnetic pulling power in Jesus command, and seen an attractive quality in this man. So much so they had simply left everything and had indeed 'followed Christ'. That had been many months ago. Now Jesus was more explicit. *'If you are going to follow me, then turn your back on yourself, take up your cross, and only then will you be fully equipped to follow me'* **(Mark 8.34).** The cross was utterly feared in ancient times as the instrument of death. Jesus died on the cross but rose again from the dead. He transformed the cross from being an instrument of death into the symbol of life. The cross of the crucified Christ was the central message in Paul's preaching.

'I decided to know nothing among you except Jesus Christ and him crucified **(1 Corinthians 2.2).** When Jesus commands us to 'take up our cross' he indicates that our witness shall be shaped by his own life and passion. In other words our Christian life will be cross-shaped. The cross sets Christians apart. *'But far be it for me to glory except in the cross of our Lord Jesus Christ by which the world has been crucified unto me, and I to the world'* **(Galatians 6.14).**

A Prayer

Heavenly Father
> Are we ready to take up our cross and follow the Master?
>> Is our ear obedient to heed that command *'Follow me'*?
>> **(Mark 1.17)**
>> Is our will submissive to your will as was Christ's in the Garden?
> *'Not my will but yours be done'* **(Matthew 26.39).**

Heavenly Father
> Prepare us, make us ready to take up that cross and follow the Master
>> we stand at the narrow gate,
>>> but we are frightened, it is shaped like a cross
> *'I stand at the door and knock. If anyone will open...*
> **(Revelation 3.20).**
> We stand at the gate and knock, hoping it will remain closed

Heavenly Father
> Receive us, for we will take up the Christ-given cross
> We will carry it on our shoulders
> And love in our heart the Carpenter who fashioned it

6   JESUS' CROSS

St. Francis of Assisi is one of my heroes.   He used three tools in his work and ministry, chastity, poverty, and obedience. Renouncing all wealth and privilege, he devoted his life to care and comfort for the sick and needy. His obedience to Christ was complete. His love for the Master knew no bounds. He went to Egypt in 1223 and preached before the sultan, gaining better treatment and conditions for the Christians under the sultan's rule. St. Francis also gained for his order the privilege of guarding the Holy Sepulchre. In 1224 he came so close to Jesus in an ecstasy of prayer that the nail prints, the stigmata, of the wounds on Jesus appeared in his own hands. When we carry our cross the very marks of Jesus' passion will appear in our soul.

John's Gospel stands in marked distinction to the other three – Synoptic – Gospels.   In the passion narrative we see one such difference. In John's Gospel we read, *'And they took Jesus and he went out, bearing his own cross, to the place called the place of the skull, Golgotha'* **(John 19.17).** But in the three Synoptic Gospels (Mark, Matthew and Luke) we read that the Roman soldiers forced a civilian to carry our Lord's cross. When a civilian felt the flat side of a Roman soldier's spear across his shoulders, then he knew he had been constrained into service. *'And they compelled a passer-by, Simon of Cyrene, to carry Christ's cross '* **(Mark 15.21).**

Both narratives are valid and each account teaches us a fundamental lesson. First only Jesus can carry the cross of our salvation, and on that cross the *'unbearable burden'* (Karl Barth) of our sin and wretchedness. But if we will be followers and witnesses for Jesus then we must carry Christ's cross in our life as if it were our own. Jesus himself taught us, *'If anyone will come after me, first let him deny himself take up his cross, and then follow me'* **(Mark 8 34).** What was it like for Simon of Cyrene when he was thrust into the centre of that scene and compelled to help this crucified Nazarene on the way to his execution and painful death? Simon saw the weakened Jesus stagger under the crushing weight of the cross. As he bent down to raise the cross beam from Christ's shoulders, did their eyes met? Did Jesus speak to him, *'Thank you Simon, you will find my yoke is easy and my burden light?'* **(Matthew 11.28-30).** And so it was for Simon. The searing heat of the midday sun bearing down on Jesus' head was for Simon like a heavenly radiance. The jeering crowd mocking Jesus sounded in Simon's ears like a host from heaven. The cross, which bore so heavily on Jesus' bent shoulders, seemed to carry Simon forward.

There is only one cross and it belongs to Christ. We are allowed to carry it, as if it were our own. Jesus carried the heavy cross of our wretchedness and sin. When we carry Jesus' cross it is full of grace, it is *'a yoke that is easy and a burden that is light'.* Samuel Rutherford wrote, *'When Jesus asks us to carry his cross Jesus always carries the heavier end'.*

(a) The Cross of Service

Then how will we carry the Easter's cross of faith? We carry three crosses, each one increasing in size and importance. The first is the cross of service. *'We live in history, and history as we know it began with Christ and was founded on the Gospels'. The gospels tell us two great truths. First, love to one's neighbour, and second life regarded as a sacrifice'* (Boris Pasternak, 'Dr Zhivago'). Pasternak the communist enunciated Christianity's deep truth. If we will be Easter Christians then we must carry our cross of service. Most people ask what they can get out of life. Christians ask what they can put into life **(Acts 20.35).** In the early decades of the Christian era the young fledgling Christian community was first persecuted then accepted, was first mocked and then respected, and through that respect it increased. The pagan Roman Empire witnessed Christians caring for their sick and elderly, burying their dead, and liberating the slave population. Julian, a bitter opponent of the Christian community, had to admit, *'The godless Galileans nourish our poor in addition to their own, while ours get no care from us'.* Christianity brought service and caring into the world, and through their service won respect. The church also raised moral standards. *'The Gospel thus became a social message'* (Harnack).

A Prayer

> *'For the Son of man came, not to be served but to serve and give his life a ransom for all'* **(Matthew 20.28)**

Gentle God
Open our eyes to see the road of service
 as the pathway to freedom
Widen our outlook to understand
 our service makes us strong
Deepen our heart that we will freely serve with love
For if we will help we must give
If we will comfort
 we must ourselves suffer
We offer ourselves
 to be Christ's ransom for others
For if we will act as a good Samaritan **(Luke 10. 29-37).**
 then we must first bend low and kneel in the dust
To find Jesus kneeling there beside us
For Jesus came

'Not to be served but to serve
and to give his life a ransom for all'

(b)   The Cross of Sacrifice

The second cross we carry is the cross of suffering and sacrifice. We talk of the passion of our Lord. 'Passion' from the Latin 'passio' has two meanings. First, our Lord suffered extreme physical pain. At Easter we remember the infinite agony Jesus endured on the cross. Crucifixion was designed to inflict the maximum amount of physical pain prior to death. But 'passion' also speaks of the mental pain and emotional anguish suffered by our Lord on the cross. That he felt deserted by man and by God his Father was a spiritual ordeal for our Redeemer We are asked to carry the cross of suffering and sacrifice for Jesus. It is only when we share someone's pain that they can feel our passion for them, that is our com-passion Only our deepest feelings can break down the barriers of distress to bring comfort and relief. But, the cross of suffering and sacrifice will hurt us. A wise minister once said to me, 'When we appear before Christ the great Shepherd of the sheep, the Lord will not ask us how many sermons we preached. Rather he will ask to see our scars and wounds'.

A Prayer

Gentle God

'He was wounded for our transgressions and bruised for our iniquities
His chastisement made us whole, by his scars we are healed' **(Isaiah 53.5)**

If by his scars we are healed

will you make the scars we carry your means of healing?
then pain is eased, and souls are comforted

If his punishment made us whole

then bear down upon us with the weight of sorrow

'For we will carry one another's burdens' **(Galatians 6.2).**

and count that weight a blessing

Our Lord did say, *'Blessed are you who carry life's burden you shall be comforted'* **(Matthew 5.4).**

If Christ was bruised for our iniquities

Then look at these scars in our soul, and stripes on our shoulders
our little stigmata marks from the cross
Gladly we carry them for the Wounded One

(c)   The Cross of Salvation

The third and final cross we carry is the cross of salvation. We are supremely Christ-like when we carry the cross of salvation. Christ's Easter cross is the cross of saving grace. By that cross God through his Son liberates the human race from evil and sin and renews men and women in the new life of salvation. But when we carry Jesus' cross in our life then Jesus will use us for the purpose of salvation. Through us, if we are faithful, Christ will continue to liberate men and women. Through us Christ will mediate his saving grace to heal and restore, to save and renew. Through us Christ will save. St. Francis prayed 'Make me a channel of your peace'. Christ will still make us channels of his peace, his saving grace, his healing mercy, his salvation as we humbly carry our cross

> *'Take up thy cross', the Saviour said,*
> *If thou wouldst my disciples be;*
> *Take up thy cross with willing heart,*
> *And humbly follow after me'*

A Dynamic Bond

We are touching the dynamic core of Christian experience. Jesus creates a living bond with his believers. Through that bond Christ gives himself to his believers. We share in Christ's life and in the saving passion of his death and resurrection. So, by carrying our cross we are carrying Jesus' cross. For there is only one cross, and it belongs to the Carpenter of Nazareth. But the passion and suffering Jesus suffered on the cross of Calvary, likewise the full extent of his rising from the dead are given to us and communicated to others as we carry our cross for the Lord.   Our cross-carrying witness can be saving witness, because Jesus uses our cross to touch and speak, to heal and save those before whom we live and witness. *'We preach Christ crucified.   Christ the power of God and the wisdom of God'* **(1 Corinthians 1.23-24).**

There can be no greater purpose to which we bend our life than carrying the cross of Christ

'We always carry in the body the death of Jesus
So that the life of Jesus may also be manifested in our bodies.'
(2 Corinthians 4.10)

A Meditation

To be Christ's and his alone
 A vision higher yet higher still
A dream fulfilled, yet ever dawning into new wonders
 A goal to strive for, and in that very struggle, achieve
A guiding destiny, as a pillar of cloud by day
 and of fire by night **(Exodus 13.21)**
Christ's passion to share until we are emptied
 and in that emptiness be fulfilled
A cross to carry on our shoulders
 to love in our heart
  to carry with us always
Until we lay it down at his nail-pierced feet

One Word in Conclusion

We all receive but one life. Its span and contents, achievements and reverses are determined by a wide variety of factors. These factors vary in importance and influence. Over some the individual person exercises a degree of control, while others shape the person and inform his outlook. We can add to our life, develop its talents, mould or distort its shape. Every person has the choice to use or abuse that God-given life, to construct or destroy with life's talents, to develop or neglect that latent ability

But the supreme personal career, the finest use for the talents of the hand, the loftiest wisdom to attract the mind, the purest affection to win the love of the heart, the holiest undertaking to liberate the soul. All of these, and countless other blessings are found when a person bends his life to the will of God, opens his days in service for Jesus, and lives in that Spiritual union with Father and Son. To be with God is the greatest use to which we can devote our life
AMEN

Chapter 3

THE DARK SIDE OF THE SOUL

For I have learned
To look on Nature, not as in the hour
Of thoughtless youth; but hearing often times
The still sad music of humanity,
Not harsh nor grating, though of ample power
To chasten and subdue

(William Wordsworth – Lines above Tintern Abbey)

1 THE DARK SIDE OF THE SOUL

On the 20 July 1969 Neil Armstrong and Bus Aldrin walked on the moon. Michael Collins, the third astronaut on Apollo 11, remained behind in the command module. The two moon walkers were exposed to great danger. But for Collins, alone in that space module, a more demanding experience lay before him. There was no car park for his space capsule as he waited for the returning moon walkers. Instead he had to orbit the moon, at the correct speed in order to rendezvous with his two companions. This meant a circumnavigation around the dark side of the moon. During that time he was totally isolated from his two colleagues, and completely out of contact with mission control at NASA. He was alone in space, isolated in the Universe. He was the first, and to this day, only person to be entirely alone in the universe. He 'saw' the dark side of the moon, everyone can experience the dark side of the soul

An incident in the life of Jacob describes the occasion when he was alone in eternity. Jacob was to meet Esau his estranged brother. In fear he despatched his family across the ford Jabbock **(Genesis 32.22-23)**. Then we read a simple sentence.

'And Jacob was left alone' **(Genesis 32.24)**. Jacob was alone on the dark side of the soul. During that dark night Jacob was alone with his memories, the irredeemable deceit perpetrated against his blind father. Jacob felt alone and apprehensive at the thought of meeting his brother. Jacob was alone with his own conscience. But ultimately, Jacob was alone with God. He was alone in eternity. We all know how he felt.

'Jacob was left alone, and a man wrestled with him until the breaking of the day' **(Genesis 32.24)**. The Old Testament writers did not use abstract language. Rather they thought in concrete pictures. So we read, 'Jacob wrestled with a man'. That man could represent his lifetime experiences, or the struggles of his own conscience. But in the last analysis this picture shows Jacob as he struggled to come to terms with his God-given destiny.

Everyone at some time in life experiences the dark side of the soul, when, like Michael Collins, we are totally alone in the personal universe that is our own life.

St. John of the Cross was a Spanish mystic and poet. He helped St. Teresa of Avila to form the Carmelite Order. One of his famous books is called 'The Dark Night of the Soul'. We have all lain awake during the dark hours of the night. For we all know the struggles in the 'dark side of our soul'.

We read that Jacob struggled with his opponent throughout the night, and with dawn breaking the man sought to escape from Jacob's grip *'Only after you bless me'* **(Genesis 32.26)**. The man from God did bless Jacob by giving him a new name. *'Your name shall no longer be called Jacob but Israel'* **(Genesis 32.28)**. The name Israel comes from two Hebrew words. 'Isra' means to strive or struggle. 'El' is the Hebrew word for God. Because that night *'Jacob strove with man and God and prevailed'* **(Genesis 32 28)**. How often we yearn for God's blessing of peace and security. But often we have to struggle to gain these spiritual blessings. Wearied by the nights of tears, tired with incessant worry, we wonder what the new day will bring. Like Jacob we have had to cope with our all too human experiences and our spiritual dilemmas before we gain a blessing

Our story ends with Jacob emerging from that destiny-filled night of the soul. But he walked away limping, because the man of God had touched his thigh **(Genesis 32.25 and 31)**. On many occasions our experiences leave us wounded and hurt. A lurking memory, a traumatic experience we will take with us to our grave. Every so often such thoughts will return to hurt us with haunting freshness. But nurse them and try to let these wounding memories rest in peace

You too can see God in the dark side of the soul. For during these challenging times God remains with you. For Jacob, now Israel, called the brook by another name **(Genesis 32.22)**. He called it Peniel. Again this name is composed of two Hebrew words. 'Peni' means the face. 'El' means God. 'Jacob called the place Peniel. For I have seen God face to face' **(Genesis 32.30)**. Jacob realised that God had been beside him, and within him. You too can see God in the dark side of the soul'.

A Prayer

'Eternal God, our God and Father in Jesus
In times of brightness and hours of light
    The eyes of faith can see you
    And you are loved in our heart of faith
But as the night follows the day
    So we must walk through the dark hours of the soul
    And live in the dark side of the soul
Support us that we will not fear
    The dark side of the soul
    Memories will frighten us
    Apprehension makes us tremble
We will be afraid
    We will call to Jesus in the boat
    'Do you not care that we perish?'
    We cry out aloud, fearing he is asleep **(Matthew 8.24).**
When we live in the dark side of the soul
Tell us
    'The Lord who keeps us neither slumbers nor sleeps'
    'The darkness is not dark to our Lord
    'The darkness is as light with God' **(Psalm 121)**
Then we shall be in peace
Through Jesus Christ
AMEN

2   THE SOLITUDE OF THE SOUL

Emil Brunner (1889-1966), the Swiss theologian was the professor of theology at Zurich University from 1924-1955. A contemporary of his more famous fellow-countryman Karl Barth, he wrote many profound books. In one of his greatest books, 'The Mediator', Brunner speaks of God coming to the individual believer in 'The solitude of his soul'. That is such a rich idea. One is reminded of Shakespeare's lines in 'Henry V' , 'I and my bosom must converse awhile and then I would no other company'.

There are times when we want no other company. These can be simple and ordinary occasions, or dramatic and challenging experiences. How many of us enjoy our worship in church and chapel because this is our personal time and space with God. Daily devotions at the beginning and end of the day are precious moments. They allow us to converse with our heart and soul, and God is our welcomed companion. Such peace-filled moments allow us the opportunity to regain our inner composure after being upset. Or we can ease the pain in a wounded soul with the healing of remembered kindnesses. Or, we can get things into true perspective after we have made a mountain out of a molehill.

Jesus welcomed these occasions when he could be alone in the solitude of his own thoughts and prayers. *'In the morning Jesus went to a lonely place to pray'* **(Mark 1.35).** At the break of day Jesus prepared himself in a deep divine communion with God his heavenly Father. In order to break into the loneliness of lost souls Jesus must first find peace in his own soul. In order to bear the heat and burden of the day as the needy crowd pressed hard, Jesus must first find his own peace in the 'solitude of his soul'.

Finally at the end of the day, Jesus again sought serenity with God his Father.

'Jesus made his disciples get into the boat while he dismissed the crowd. Afterwards he went up into the hill by himself to pray' **(Matthew 14.22-23).** Now if Jesus used these personal times at the start and close of the day, then we should follow our Lord's example. More, if Jesus required these personal moments of solitude, can we dispense with them? In the frenetic pace of life, we have lost our inner tranquillity. One hymn captures that moment when the hush of the evening brings peace and rest to the business of the day.

'O Sabbath rest by Galilee!
O calm of hills above,
Where Jesus knelt to share with thee
The silence of eternity,
Interpreted by love

Paul Tillich's volumes of sermons are thought provoking. In one sermon, entitled 'Loneliness and Solitude', he wrote, 'Loneliness express the pain of being alone, solitude expresses the glory of being alone' ("The Eternal Now" page 11). We can readily understand these words for they have often described our own experiences. We have often tasted the pain of loneliness instead of the peace of solitude. We cannot avoid these personal events nor escape from such feelings. They rush upon us from many directions. They are hidden in different guises. Tennyson speaks for many of us, *'The tender grace of a day that is dead will never come back to me'*.

Under these circumstances we feel isolated, and suspect people do not understand us. But there is One who does understand, standing beside us he will keep us from falling. For Jesus himself tasted the bitter pain of loneliness. If on the hillside Jesus felt the nearness of his eternal Father, then the night would come when the peaceful solitude would turn into a painful loneliness. In the Garden of Gethsemane, on the night when Jesus was betrayed, Jesus prayed in abandoned loneliness. *'Father, let this cup pass from me'* **(Matthew 26.36-46).** God spoke to Elijah in the *'still small voice of calm'* **(1 Kings 19.12).** At the empty tomb Jesus broke into the silence of her soul by pronouncing Mary's name **(John 20.11-18).** Jesus will break into your silence and share your lonely walk. Jesus will call to you by your own name.

> *'I am the Good Shepherd. The sheep hear my voice.*
> *I call them, I call you, by name and lead you out'* **(John 10.1-6).**

A Prayer

Dear God and Father
> In a moment but not belonging to time
> a place unrestricted by space
> we can know loneliness, the loneliness of the soul, our soul

We can be alone as if the world were empty
Our loneliness can be dark
Dream-filled, shadows flit across our mind
> memories revived, fresh as at their first occurrence
> and with the memory a hurt, as sore now as it was then.

Our loneliness can be lonesome
> for none do return who have left us

Our loneliness is regretful
For none can undo the deed
> nor re-write the script we wrote

The loneliness of our soul
Where none can enter, feel its moment
 none but the lonely heart
Gentle God
 By your presence
 transform our loneliness into solitude
 for the solitude of the soul is your presence
For you enter
 You feel with us, for us
The solitude of the soul is your comfort
 For you touch the wound refusing healing
 You speak to the silence deaf to hearing
 You love the heart beyond loving
 You trust the soul with no believing
Who is that companion
 turning grey loneliness into bright solitude
 if it be not Jesus
Whose the comfort if not the One who knew
 neither companion, nor comfort
In the loneliness of the Cross

3 ILL FOR THIRTY-EIGHT YEARS

Many people are struck down with debilitating illnesses, confined to home or wheelchair, aware their natural abilities are now severely restricted. These illnesses strike at the heart of every family, colour each day, govern family plans. The careers of many young people are immediately arrested. Family resources, especially financial funds, are suddenly strained, depleted, and used in different ways. Other members in the family sacrifice their own futures and prospects to meet the demands of a radically altered domestic situation. Such personal responses are stimulated by unselfish love and generous care. But these illnesses cause deep and lasting emotional changes, from hope of cure to the disappointment when none was forthcoming, from inner frustration to expressed hostility. The emotional consequences can be traumatic. This small meditation is dedicated to them. For those who have a fit body with the physical freedom of action and movement must be forever grateful for life's greatest gift of health, must never abuse that healthy body, nor ever forget the ones whose mind is yearning but whose body is weak.

Based on John 5.1-9

Today will be like yesterday, like all these other yesterdays
How many yesterdays to make a year?
But not just one year, thirty eight now.
Every day will be the same. What does it matter now?
They say there is a cure in this pool,
    No use for me. Always someone before me.
    I used to be at the rim ready to roll into that pool.
    Then one night while I slept they moved me back.
    Now I can scarcely see the pool. I'm in a long waiting list.
I've stopped thinking about my younger days.
    I've stopped thinking, feeling, being upset.
    What's the point? Nobody wants to hear your moans and groans.
    Suppose that's why the family stopped coming a long time
    ago, haven't seen them for months.
    Look at me, these rags, these dirty rags,
    My shroud, if only it could be. Better dead than this lot.
    They stole my warm blanket the night they shifted me.
It wasn't always like this. I had a good life ahead of me.
    I had a trade, I was strong, I was good at my job.
    I had a girl friend. We were going to get married.
    Then one day, that tingling in my hand,
    Didn't think much of it at first, it had been a long day, just tired.
    But it got worse.
    Got that I couldn't hold my tools. Whatever happened to them.
    He took them, he always had his eye on them.
    Then the accident. I dropped the end of the wood, nearly
        killed him, that was the end for me.
That was a long time ago,
    Nearly thirty-eight years ago. Or something like that,
    I don't know. What does it matter, nothing matters now.
    They put me here, said they would keep watch to roll me into
    the pool.
    "Take turns", they said.
At first it worked, and I could struggle for myself.

Then they drifted off and I got worse.
Can't blame them, they have their lives to live.
She got married.
Don't get me wrong. I don't blame her one bit.
Who wants to get married to me?
That was a long time ago, thirty-eight years to be exact.
Here they come, they are back.
The mob, last time they said I had cheated their friend
Moved in front of him.
So they moved me back here, probably took my blanket
That's a laugh! I can't move at all.
Said it was for my own good, to teach me a lesson.
Don't need it. Life has taught me my lesson
A bitter, bitter lesson.
I know now that life can be cruel and people are not interested.
It's lonely here at nights
And it's cold, that's when the pain gets worse.
Yes, I'm angry, frustrated, resentful and bitter.
Don't try and tell me otherwise.
If you had been here for thirty-eight years
You would know all about it
You have a life to enjoy
You can walk away from this place, from me.
Don't say you are sorry, then walk away.
Stop. Look at me.
Have you any idea what this is like?
Don't talk to me about God
Where is God all this time?
Pray, I gave that up a long time ago.
What was God doing when I prayed to Him?
And I used to pray, real deep, real tears, real prayers.
What was God doing when I prayed like that?
This is a different mob.
Haven't seen this lot. What does he want?
Get better, of course I want to get better.
Think I enjoy being here like this.
Get up. I wish I could!

Try, I've been trying all the time
O.K. Here goes.
I'm standing! I'm standing!!
Now walk, "Walk? Yes, walk".
I'm walking! I'm walking!!
I'm standing and I'm walking!
Trouble is, it's thirty-eight years too late for me.

A Prayer

Gentle God
We pray to you in body, with mind, and from the soul
We cherish the priceless gift of health and strength
So easily forgotten, so often abused
Gentle God
In utter humility we ask
Will you strengthen, encourage, and remain
With your children
In every moment of their thirty eight years

4   UNANSWERED PRAYER

"Be not silent, O God of my praise" **(Psalm 109.1)**
"To Thee, O Lord I call
My rock, be not deaf to me
Lest, if Thou be silent to me,
I become like those who go down to the pit" **(Psalm 28.1).**

It is said that no prayer remains unanswered, but "shopping list" prayers may be disappointed. Again it is taught that the power of prayer lies not in what it "gives" to a person but rather in what it "does" to a person. But from the perspective of the devout, worshipping, believer, many prayers appear to go unanswered. It is an age-long dilemma encountered when trust and worship are confronted with the impenetrable wall of silence. As the believing psalmist wrote, "Be not silent, O God of my praise". It is the God of his praise who remains silent. But unanswered prayer is personal and immediate, especially in times of deep distress. The apparent unwillingness or inability of God to respond to the cry from the broken heart – even with the gift of peace - can often plunge the praying soul into deep despair. Again, the psalmist wrote, " If Thou be silent to me, I become like those who plunge into the pit". That pit can be deep, dark and dangerous.

A Meditation

"Hallowed be your name, O God, on earth as in Heaven.
    Hallowed be your name"
Holy indeed is God
    God of my worshipping soul
    God of the care and cure of my very existence.
Holy indeed is my God
    Hallowed ever in my prayers
Even to utter these simple and familiar words
    Is prayer
        and from prayer blessing
            and in blessing peace
    "There is a river
    the streams whereof shall make glad
    the city of God' **(Psalm 46.4).**
That city of God is my soul
    The streams of blessing
        released by prayer
            shall gladden my soul.
    "Ask what ye will in My Name
    And the Father shall give it unto you' **(John 15.16).**
Joyfully my soul asks of the gentle and generous
    Godly Father and Fatherly God
That there will be a gentle healing
    for that hurt in soul and spirit
        an easing of wound to body and soul
        respite from pain
Prayer messenger bring that healing to me
    that I can hold it to my wounded soul
Praise be to God
    For that tender presence
        in the darkness of the night
When fears invade through cover of darkness
    not the darkness of the night
        but the deeper darkness of the soul

Praise be to God for that tender presence
    in the darkness of the night
Praise be to God
    who hears the prayers without words
Hannah's prayers too deep for words
    too personal for others to hear
        only meant for God
Praise be to God
    who responds with a blessing
        deeper still than the depth of soul's despair
            and responds with a deep inner peace
"The peace of God that passes all understanding
keeping secure guard over heart and soul
through Christ Jesus" **(Philippians 4.7).**
"Your will be done on earth – in my soul-
    As in heaven"
    For my prayers fall into the strong hands of God
        who controls my life
    For my soul is kept by you, loving God
        whose children can cry and be heard
    And blessed
"Your will be done on earth" – in my soul
"Hallowed be your Name"
    utters my prayer
        for there is blessing
            and in blessing a healing
                and from healing a peace
                    in peace rest for the soul.
If only it were so.
    How I yearn for these things
    They are far from me, I have not touched them
    They are distant from me. I have not felt them
For me, only a lingering silence.

5   SILENCE

Silence is misunderstood by all, feared by the many, but familiar to those of deep spirits. Silence is the language of messages without words, where no audible sound is required to communicate.

We enter this world of silence and will encounter an uncompromising challenge to our emotions. But the challenge is accompanied by a unique opportunity. For silence allows us to penetrate into deeper thoughts and unexplored feelings. We speak here of a silence in the midst of sound, wherein those who can communicate with spoken words choose not to, because they do not need to confident that their thoughts will be understood in silence.

Silence is also the second language of God, through which God speaks to us. For the same God and Father of Jesus Christ, who said "Let there be light and there was light", the same God who spoke to us in Jesus Christ the living Word of God – the living audible voice and sound of God- also speaks to us in silence and in the world of "no-word-silence".

A Meditation

The Silence of God
 is heard most clearly in the Garden of Gethsemane
"My children
 Do not be afraid when you hear only my silence
 It does not mean that I no longer speak to you
I speak to you in different ways
 and often in the language of silence
Listen to my silent conversation
 listen to my silent one-ness with my Jesus
  in the garden called Gethsemane
 We were at-one with each other
  in a one-ness achieved only through silence.
There in that silence
I did not rebuff my Son
 nor turn hostile without feeling
I did not listen with a cold heart
 Unfeeling
No, rather, these words of Jesus
 "Father, let this cup pass from my lips" **(Luke 22.42).**
 broke my heart, broke my soul

Dear children, the heart of Your Eternal God and Father
    hurts longer
    because I hurt eternally
Dear children, the pain in my soul is more penetrating
    because I am for you holy, that is, pure

For your sakes I must be eternal
    to gather up your time
For your sakes I must be pure and holy
    to heal you of all your wounds
These Sonly words of Jesus were so deep
    "Father, let this cup pass from my lips"
That I could only answer Jesus with silence
    only my eternal silence could respond to my Son.
In that silence
    I broke my heart
    in order to strengthen his
    I was crucified in my soul
        before my Son was crucified on his cross

Dear children
    Do not grieve at my silence
    My silence is my message to you
        deeper still than any spoken word
        communicating something of eternity
    Do not fear my silence
        it is my way of speaking to you
    At this time

Dear God
    Dear gentle Father, our life in Jesus, Your Son
    Do not fear our silence
        do not be afraid when you hear only our silence
Like Hannah of old **(1 Samuel 1.12-18)**
    Whose lips moved to the feelings of the heart
        but whose lips were incapable of expressing
    These silent feelings with audible words.
So she prayed with moving lips
    heart-created prayers

with silent words
with silence
In like manner
Do we pray in silence
do not be afraid when you hear only our silence
Do not fear that we have turned away from Jesus
to whom we forever belong
who has made us new
saved us
And with whom we forever live a sacramental life

We cry in pain and prayer
we trust each other
we share sacramentally gentleness and tears.
We turn unto you constantly
we turn unto you less often
You hear only our diminishing voice
then our silence
Gentle God, do not fear when you hear
As you have heard
only silence.
For, Heavenly Father
Pain increases, distress deepens
devotion stumbles
old devotion cannot carry the burden of the soul

We were taught how to pray, believe, trust
but these old ways were broken and cast to the ground
We stopped using them
we used only our silence

Dear Father, do not be afraid when you hear only our silence.
Our silence is our prayer
deeper than expressed words
Our silence is our trust
reaching out to a greater Jesus
Our silence is our devotion
for we still love you
Our silence is our believing

for we still depend upon you
Our silence is our surrender
    for we still follow in the footsteps of Jesus
- nail pierced footsteps

Dear Father, God
Do not fear when you hear only our silence
    "Out of the depths I cry to Thee, O Lord!
    Lord, hear my voice" **(Psalm 130.1).**
Dear Father
    May Jesus take our prayer-less-ness into his praying
    'I pray for all who believe in me' **(John 17.20)**
Then our prayerlessness
    becomes our prayer-full-ness, in silence
May Jesus hear the prayers of an empty heart
    now silent because it is empty
    now empty because it is so sore
May Jesus bless the silent soul
    for the silence of our soul
    is our answer
    to the silence we have heard for so long
The silence that comes from our Father God
    do not fear when you hear only our silence.

Bless us Father God
    With a silent blessing
    For such a blessing comes from the silence of God
We shall answer with the silence of the soul
    'Bless the Lord, O, my soul
    And all that is within me, bless his holy name' **(Psalm 103.1).**

6 THICK DARKNESS

'Moses went into the thick darkness where God was' **(Exodus 20.21)**

In the Bible light signifies God's presence. Darkness on the other hand was the realm without the presence of God. Hence it was the realm of evil. When the people stood apart and allowed Moses to enter the dark cloud over Sinai they were convinced he was lost forever. He had entered the realm of darkness. But the Exodus narrative tells another story. Moses entered the thick darkness - and there was God! **(Exodus 20.21)** We have all entered the cloud of thick darkness. The memory of its deep shadow still frightens us. We are afraid when we are *'walking through the valley of deepest darkness'* **(Psalm 23.4).** Our fears are well grounded, and our feelings are a natural reaction. When it is our turn in life to enter the cloud of thick darkness, may we discover like Moses that God is already there.

A Meditation

Father God
It is dark, our ambushed souls take fright.
    we cannot see the way ahead, we are alarmed
    we cannot see each other, we are frightened
We cannot see Jesus, we are desolate.
We enter the thick darkness
    of unfamiliar distress and unrecognised suffering
Nobody can imagine our horror, share our darkness
    feel our pain, experience that emotion

If we be your Moses to enter that darkness
Be our Moses-God to meet us there
Seen by us you will not be
    seen by you we will be
Held by us you cannot be
    grasped by you from falling we shall forever be

We enter the thick darkness so dark that it threatens
    nay denies us, denies us life itself
    then denies us God – God himself
Be our God in that darkness
    meet us there, embrace us in the shadow
    support us from the fall
Be our God in that darkness
    deny the darkness with its power and threat
Be our God, affirm you are our God
    and thus defeat the darkness around us and within us

Affirm you are God
    then confirm we are yours

alive and safe in you
in light, in him who is the light of the world **(John 8.12)**

He knew that darkness
where he thought there was no God
no Father
'Eli, Eli, lama sabachthami'
'My God, my God why hast thou forsaken me?' **(Mark 15.34).**
and left me in darkness

He knows that darkness, and feels its fright
may he be with us, we know he is with us
'We enter the thick darkness, where we fear to be alone
Lord Jesus be with us, be our Light

The deepest darkness was yet to come
*'When the sixth hour had come, there was darkness over
the whole land until the ninth hour. At the ninth hour Jesus
cried with a loud voice, 'Eloi, Eloi, lama sabachthani'. 'My
God, my God, why hast thou forsaken me'* **(Matthew 27.45-46)**

Deepest darkness.
darkness from evil's dark dungeon
bursting forth to cover the whole land in darkness
that the very sun lost its light
and the lights in the Celestial City flickered.
Darkness from the black heart of evil
laid claim to Him who was the Light of life
the Light shone in darkness and darkness
extinguished it

But from the deepest darkness came a radiance most pure
For the second Moses, the Light of life
went into the thick darkness of that other Sinai
Our Calvary
and there was God
'Twas that meeting
of God in whom there is no darkness
with Him who is the Light of life
in the radiance Spirit
That is our salvation.

74

For we are buried with Jesus into his dying, into darkness
To be raised with Jesus in his resurrection to life, to light
(Romans 6.4)
'Lux perpetua luceat eius'. 'Let perpetual light shine upon them'. **(The 'Communio' from Mozart's Requiem)**

7   UNWANTED

Mother Teresa of Calcutta (1910-1997) was a wonderful example and inspiration to everyone irrespective of race or creed.   In 1948 she left the convent of the Loreto Sisters to work alone in the slums of Calcutta. She realised how much the slum dwellers required medical help as well as spiritual comfort. So she went to Paris for medical training. In 1950 on her return she established her sisterhood, the Missionaries of Charity, and two years later in 1952 her house for the dying was opened. Five years later she embarked on her work among the lepers. No other individual has won the admiration of the world; and shown what Christian faith and love when sealed by spiritual obedience can achieve. Little wonder that Mother Teresa was awarded the Pope John XXIII Peace Prize in 1971, the inaugural Templeton Prize for Progress in Religion in 1973 and the Nobel Peace Prize in 1979.

That is why the recently published private papers of Mother Teresa will astonish, if not frighten, many believers. In the volume 'Come Be My Light' these published letters and papers reveal an inner struggle and agony she endured for many decades. Her deep agony was the sense of being unwanted. To be unwanted is the utmost experience of personal negation. To be made redundant tells the person that some firm does not want the skills of hand and training of mind. To be retired speaks to that person that age has caught up with him. But, to be unwanted is the worst fate of all

While I was a young minister in the Highlands I led the search and rescue team linked to the Mountain Rescue Team in Ross and Cromarty Police Force. The search and rescue members were additional to the core Police unit. But they were shepherds and gillies, whose knowledge of the hills was invaluable. One afternoon we were called out. But I was the only member of the search and rescue team, the others were at their work. A car, abandoned for a day, alerted the police of an accident or tragedy. Word came through that a man from the west of Scotland had been reported missing, and his was the abandoned car. The mountain demanded technical training I did not possess, so the trained police officers searched the mountains recesses. I was asked to search an area of moor land criss-crossed by ditches and streams. In one of these ditches I discovered the body. An empty bottle of spirits and a medicine container for tablets lay on the heather As I waited for the police team to come to the scene, my heart grieved for the poor man. What feelings drove him to these extremes. Did he feel unwanted by life?

But to be unwanted by God, that is a deeper and more demanding experience, as Mother Teresa suffered. In her work and example Mother Teresa showed the fullness of Christ. But in her inner life she knew only emptiness and God forsakenness. She felt unwanted. Did Judas feel unwanted by Christ, that in the end he committed suicide?

On the night when Jesus was betrayed – by Judas – he gave to his disciples the rite of the Last Supper, the Sacrament of Communion or the Mass. But Jesus offered a dire warning to the person by whose actions he was to be betrayed.

'The Son of Man goes as it is written of him, but woe to that man by whom the Son of man is betrayed. It would have been better for that man if he had not been born' **(Matthew 26.24).**

We know that the disciples fled from Jesus and left him in the lurch. We also know that Peter hovered around in the temple courtyard, unable to help Jesus, equally unable to stay away. Did Judas hover in the precincts of the temple, anxious about the outcome of the events precipitated by his act of betrayal? Suppose during the night in the shuttling back and forward from temple to praetorian headquarters Judas saw Jesus and their eyes met. What look could have passed from Jesus to Judas? Did Judas see in Jesus' gaze that he was now unwanted by the Son of God? Or did Jesus smile at Judas, still wanting him, already forgiving him? Because only a few hours earlier Jesus had smiled at Judas wanting him to stay. Only a few steps away in the Upper Room Jesus had deliberately singled out Judas to receive that first sacramental piece, and in that gesture opened his heart and yearned for him to remain with them **(John 13.26-27)**.

But let us return to what was experienced by Mother Teresa. There is a profound challenge to any believer in her deep and agonising struggle. She suffered a total and absolute experience of being unwanted by God. All doors were closed and every spiritual avenue sealed against her. So much so that she felt there was no God, no soul, and no Jesus. The question thrusts itself upon us, Why should such a feeling descend upon one of such purity of soul and dedication of life such as Mother Teresa?

We are standing on the border of life's deepest mystery and the soul's most profound feeling. The nearer we come to God the heavier becomes our cross, the darker our vision, the more difficult our faith.

One could expand this contrast by saying that the closer we come to the God of light the greater we are enclosed in our own darkness. Or we could say that the closer we come to the holy God the keener we feel God's 'otherness' and our unworthiness.

But such metaphorical language does not add to but could diminish from the absolute contrast that a saint can feel unwanted by God. The clearest expression of this enormous spiritual experience is to be found in Isaiah 53. In that chapter we read that the suffering servant of the Lord fulfils Gods purpose by being-unwanted.

We are compelled to return to the cross. Not that we will discover concrete answers to satisfy the mind. Rather we will be confronted by what can only be described as 'The mystery of God'. Such an encounter will reach beyond mind to inform the soul.

For it is in the Unwanted One of Calvary that we will find that we are wanted and loved by God. This may appear foolish by human logic but it is the wisdom of the gospel and the knowledge of the cross. As Paul wrote, *'The word of the cross is folly to those who are perishing, but to those who are saved it is the power of God…..*

For the foolishness of God is wiser than people, and the weakness of God is stronger than people' **(1 Corinthians 1.18-25)**

For it is the Unwanted One on the cross who still embraces us to himself even when we are convinced that we are unwanted. But what was the response of Mother Teresa to her feelings of darkness and unwantedness?   She was convinced that Jesus had asked her, 'Come be my Light' (hence the title of her book). She was certain that Jesus wanted her to spread his light in order to dispel the darkness both within her own soul and around her in her missionary work. She took the spiritual agony of her soul and transformed it into her caring and saving work among the homeless and lepers. .

A Meditation

Heavenly Father, Gentle God
Did the eyes of Jesus look upon Peter as our Lord was led to his end
    did our Lord's eyes say to Peter, 'You do not want me
    Peter?'
    but more condemning, 'I do not want you'
But unrecorded of Jesus and Judas, did their eyes meet?
    did Judas see in Jesus' eyes, 'I do not want you'
    did Judas hear 'The Son of Man goes to his end
    but woe to him by whom he is betrayed'?
Then did Judas, the unwanted Judas, end it all?
Or, if they met in that courtyard, did Jesus smile at him?
    Jesus wanting Judas, caring and loving him
Jesus, offering to Judas his whole life
    even as he had only hours before proffered a portion of
    bread
    speaking in sacramental language 'I want you'.
On the cross was that millstone removed from Judas?

Gentle God
    Have you felt unwanted?
Gentle God,
Yours is the eternal desolation of being unwanted
I open my heart to you but you would not
    'I was ready to be sought by those who did not ask for me
    I was ready to be found by those who did not seek me
    I said, 'Here am I, Here am I'
    To a nation that did not call on my name
    I spread out my hands all the day to a rebellious people'
    (Isaiah 65.1-2).
When he died, that precious Son
    how greatly did you feel unwanted.

'God shows his love towards us
that while we are sinners Christ died for us' **(Romans 5.8)**

In Jesus
>   You healed the wounds, raised the dead, comforted the mourning
>   gave to us a new life
>   Bethlehem was your birth, Galilee your life
>   Calvary your death, and the tomb-emptied your glory

It was your very self you gave to them in Jesus

And they rejected you – unwanted - when they crucified your Son

Gentle God
>   How greatly do you feel unwanted by us
>   for this generation continues to create its Calvary
>   And in his Son, rejected and crucified,
>   tells the Father God is unwanted.

Gentle God
>   For when they say, 'They do not need Jesus'
>   they tell you the cross was unnecessary
>   Jesus died in vain, for they need him not
>   Then they shouted 'Crucify him, crucify him'
>   Now they shout 'Don't bother'
>   But, God, your passion and love
>   felt from all eternity!
>   is it all nothingness because unwanted?

Gentle God
>   Whose the greater pain?
>   for people to be unwanted by God
>   for God to be unwanted by people

'Tis yours
>   For when they reject your Son – unwanted
>   They speak to his God and Father a terrible message
>   This is your own passion and Calvary
>   But we look in vain for an empty tomb for your release

For men and women have turned away from your Son
>   we do not need his blood, his agony

it was all unnecessary
We do not want you God
are these the calls from the human heart breaking the divine
heart?

O heavenly Father
Do not turn your back upon us as we deserve
do not close your ear to our cry
nor your heart to our wretchedness
lest we be unwanted
We flee to that place where the Unwanted One still yearns for us
to take us to the God and Father the world does not want
unwanted Father God who still yearns for his children.

Chapter 4

SUMMER DAYS

'And so the Word had breath and wrought
With human hands the creed of creeds
In loveliness of perfect deeds
More strong than all poetic thought'

(Tennyson 'In Memoriam')

As a young and painfully inexperienced minister fresh from college I once met a man who taught me more with his life than professors with their learning. When he stood to pray he had already created a peaceful stillness. He brought his words from a nearer presence where I had never been. He gave to them a depth I failed to fathom. He had been somewhere with the Lord, conversing with Him, but my rough hands could not prise open the door to his inner soul-chamber. Like Moses his face shone, *'And he did not know'* **(Exodus 34.29).** Though he did protest otherwise we all saw Christ in him. In this saintly man 'The Word had breath and wrought the creed of creeds'. In his humble life there was 'A loveliness of perfect deeds, more strong than all poetic (or theological) thought'.

When we encounter someone of such maturity of soul then we are truly blessed. Because they look beyond our narrow vision they encourage us to enlarge our own. Because they firmly walk with the One who is their *'Way, truth, and life'* **(John 14.6)** they stimulate us to pass through the gate that is narrow and tread the path of faith that is hard and difficult to find **(Matthew 7. 13-14).** Because they share with us a grace-filled winsomeness they make us pause, wondering how we could ever become a Christian like them. They create summer days of happiness and peace in every season of the year.

1   THE FACE OF GOD

'I have seen your face as though I had seen the very face of God'
(Genesis 33.10)
Gentle God, Heavenly Father,
Thank you for those fine people we have met
    in whom we see the very face of God.
They are heaven-created people
    reflecting the radiance of your presence.
 Thank you for their smile,
    to brighten our little world,
    a rising sun from the eastern sky.
'I have seen your face as though I had seen the very face of God'
We look into warm eyes
    deep pools of kindness, springs of fresh affection.

We drink of the water of kindness
'A spring of love welling up from mature lives'
'I have seen your face as though I had seen the very face of God'
Firm lines cross that face
etched by an inner character.
These lines from one supporting us, caring deeply, guiding,
and in our need correcting us
'I have seen your face as though I had seen the very face of God'
'They rejoice when we rejoice, they weep with us when we cry'
(Romans 12.25)
Tears from the soul gently flow, sad, kind, abundant,
more tears in the soul than the eyes can hold.
The language of tears, often a lament
always speaks kindly
Only a gentle soul can nurse these tears
'I see your face as though I had seen the very face of God'
Thank you for their laughter,
their smile when they share our little pleasures.
They see the funny side of life
and help us to laugh once again.

Gentle God
I pray earnestly that they will see your face in my face,
that I shall be to them what they have been to me.
Mine the finger of faith pointing to Jesus
Mine the conversation as if Jesus were speaking.
Mine the heartbeat in which Jesus is loving.
The very life through which Jesus is drawing near.
For if 'I see your face as though I had seen the very face of God'
I pray, 'May they see my face as though they had seen the very face of God'
And when we shall see Christ
We shall recognise him
as though we had known him all our life.
For we have both known and met him,
his familiar face in those

'In whom we have seen the very face of God'
'O Saul it shall be a Face like my face that receives thee
A Man like me thou shalt love and be loved by, forever
A Hand like this hand shall throw open the gates of new life to thee
See the Christ stand' **(Robert Browning 'Saul')**
Look to Jesus

> *'We have looked into your eyes, Jesus, as into the eyes of
> God' 'Jesus looked upon him and loved him'* **(Mark 10.21)**

As Jesus looked kindly upon the young man
>   so these eyes have looked kindly upon us.

Jesus smiles to the sound of our laughter
>   but grieves at the sight of our tears,
>   and the sharpness of our pain.

Look to Jesus

> *'We grasp your hand, Jesus, as reaching for the hand of God'*
> *'Jesus reached out his hand and caught him'* **(Matthew 14.31)**

As Jesus pulled to safety the drowning Peter
>   So these hands stretch out and caught us,
>   your hands, we felt the nail-prints in these palms

>   Still throbbing with the pain from our weaknesses
>   still bleeding with our sins
>   still out-stretched as on a cross, our cross

Look to Jesus
We listen to Jesus and hear the very Word of God
> *'They were astonished, he taught as one with authority'*
> **(Matthew 7.29)**
> *'The still small voice'* **(1 Kings19.12)**

The very whisper of Jesus speaking
>   gives sound to God's voice beyond our hearing
>   translates the language of God's Word
>   into a diction we can understand

To whom can we go, but to the living Word, to Jesus
>   For to Jesus belong the words of wisdom
>   *'To whom can we go yours are the words of eternal life'*
>   **(John 6.68)**

Look to Jesus
>   We have heard the heart beat of love, Jesus' love,

and felt the very love of God.
God pierced the side of Adam to create another being,
but the soldier pierced the side of the Christ, our new Being.
(John 19.3)
Your heart is broken by our misery
ours is healed in your compassion.
Pained love in a broken heart from a pierc-ed side
pained love alone creates for us a new being.
Look to Jesus
We look to Jesus and we see God face to face
'Jesus was transformed before them' **(Mark 9.2)**
'Be not conformed to this world, but be ye transformed
by the renewing of your mind and soul' **(Romans 12.2)**
For when we were being shaped by the rough hands of this time
and conformed to this world
Jesus, you revealed to us our real life
Transformed before us and within us
'No one has seen God at any time.
The only Son from the Father
has made God known' **(John 1.14).**

Jesus, look at us
'No one has ever seen God. If we love one another,
God abides in us and his love is perfected in us' **(1 John 4.12)**
As you look at us, listen to our conversations,
and know our innermost thoughts.
We pray earnestly and humbly
That when you see our life
you will find something, however small, of your life.
When you look into our face
you will recognise the outline, however faint,
of the countenance of your Father God.

A Dedication

In the course of our life we meet many lovely people. A husband and wife, parents and children, brothers and sisters. But friends can become our family. **(Mark 3.34-35)**. These lovely people possess a pure soul, and this goodness radiates   throughout their life. Their words are kind, their thoughts wholesome, their actions mature. Because thought, word, and deed are inspired by their pure soul. After such a person enters our life they will remain in our heart forever. If in our life we meet one such person we are fortunate. If we encounter more than one we are truly God-blessed.

2   LIFE'S SACRED FACE

In his compelling and chilling book 'If this is Man', an account of his experiences in Auschwitz, Primo Levi recounts the incident when he reached out to grasp an icicle to quench his raging thirst only to have the guard snatch it from his hand. This was one of the many ways he realised that in the camp there would be neither kindness nor help, but only brutality and cruelty. He wrote 'No Sacred Face will help you here'. But Christians will see the Sacred Face of the Easter Jesus Christ, and can watch the face of their daily life transformed by Christ's radiance. We may often wonder if our Christian conduct makes any difference? Do our efforts to follow Christ's teachings help us and enrich the lives of friend and neighbour? We will attend church and chapel, but will anyone notice? In our daily life are we showing the 'sacred face of Jesus' to others?

We often use the word 'face' to describe our life experiences. We wonder how we will 'face up' to the new day. We put a 'brave face' on things, when we hide our inner feelings. When we do something wrong we feel 'shame-faced'. When we receive bad news our face is 'clouded' The same meaning is found in the language of the Bible. To see someone's face meant to be in that person's presence. When the psalmist pleads, *'Hide not thy face from me'* **(Psalm 27.9)** he asks that God not leave him. We often use the expression 'face to face', meaning we see someone intimately. So Paul wrote, *'(In this life) we see through a mirror dimly but (in God's life) we will see face to face, (that is clearly)'* **(I Corinthians 13.12)**

The stories of Moses meeting with God are so meaningful. When he first encountered the presence of the living God, Moses, *'Hid his face for he was afraid to look at God'* **(Exodus 3.6).** But during the wilderness journey God drew Moses closer to himself. *'The Lord used to speak to Moses face to face as a man speaks to a friend'*

(Exodus 33.11) And at the end of his life it was said of Moses, *'There has never arisen a prophet like Moses whom the Lord knew face to face'* **(Deuteronomy 34.10)** Will people speak about us in that way? There is a lovely story about the reunion of Jacob and Esau, the two estranged brother. When Jacob realised how good Esau was to him he said, *'I have seen thy face as though I had seen the face of God'* **(Genesis 33.100.**

   We can so often show the true face of life, even the sacred face of God. Our smile on meeting a friend, the look of our concern when friends speak can often indicate our deep feelings and encourage our friend in challenging times. Likewise our words can echo the sacred voice of God, and our actions reveal the sacred deeds of God. Never minimise what your words and deeds – and your smile – can achieve. You are showing the sacred face of God. There is a warm and very human dimension to such conduct. A person may not realise how helpful such conduct is proving to be for family or friend. Another instructive story narrates how Moses descended from Mount Sinai with the two tablets of stone with the Ten Commandments. We read, *'Moses did not know that the skin of his face shone because he had been talking with God'* **(Genesis 34.29).** This simple yet moving story contains a deep inner truth. Moses had been in close contact with God, hence an inner radiance shone from him, but he himself was totally unaware of his appearance. You can often have the same effect upon your friend or family member. You may be encouraging them through that terrible experience, without realising how helpful you have been. Just as Moses face shone without his knowing. Your presence and encouraging words may just have helped them to turn the corner and see light at the end of the dark tunnel. You probably showed them 'the sacred face of God'

   Sometimes we only see the darkened face of life. There are these many moments of distress and challenge when we feel that God has hidden his face from us *'How long will you hide your face from me how long must I bear pain in my soul and sorrow in my heart'* **(Psalm 13.2).** There is another encouraging story in the Bible that can help us overcome these terrible experiences when we see no sacred face but only the hostile scowl of life. The great Jacob had deceived his father into giving him the father's blessing that rightfully belonged to Esau his brother. Now he was on the point of meeting his estranged brother. But he had first to come to terms with his chequered past, make peace with his conscience and his God. He spent the night in personal and spiritual conflict **(Genesis 32.22-32)**. The Bible described that Jacob wrestled with the messenger of God all night. Jacob refused to release the angel of God until he had been blessed, so the angel of the Lord touched his thigh and put it out of joint and Jacob limped from that day onwards. But Jacob was blessed and when morning came he said, *'I have seen God face to face yet my life is preserved'* **(Genesis 32.30)**. There are these experiences from which we emerge often wounded in spirit and in soul, in heart and in mind. But these are often the very times when we see both the darker face of life and deeper into the soul of God.

But there was once a man in whose countenance we saw the 'sacred face of God'. He was Jesus of Nazareth. If we read between the lines the face of Jesus mirrored many emotions. What attracted Matthew when Jesus looked on him, so that Matthew left his office job to be a disciple? **(Matthew 9.9)**. There was a profound look of sadness on Jesus' face when the rich young man deserted him **(Mark 10.21)**. There was a look on infinite sadness when Jesus saw the grave of his friend Lazarus, and great tears flowed down that royal countenance **(John 11.33-36)**. But when Peter tried to prevent Jesus going to Jerusalem, then the look on Jesus' face reflected the eternal will of Almighty God. There are many pictures in the sacred face of Christ. When we look into the face of Jesus Christ we see the smiling face of God. But at a deeper level we can also see the radiance of the holy face of God. The sacred face of God was seen in that holy Jesus.

> *'Jesus took Peter James and John and led them apart*
> *on to a high mountain. There Jesus was transformed*
> *before them, his face shone like the sun, and his garments*
> *became white as snow'* **(Matthew 17.1-2)**

On that mount of Transfiguration the disciples were privileged to see the true meaning and shape of life, human life under the grace and mercy, peace and love of God the Father. God in his utter mercy and movement towards us in forgiving love transforms our life, renewing us sacred and pure *'Do not be conformed to this world but be ye transformed by the renewal of our soul and conscience'* **(Romans 12.1-2)**

But the day fast approached when the disciples saw another look upon the sacred face of Jesus. *'When the days drew near Jesus set his face to go to Jerusalem'* **(Luke 9.51).** There was a look of utter determination upon Jesus' countenance. Little wonder the disciples felt shivers of fear and were reluctant to enquire too deeply of the Lord.

'Jesus taught the disciples, that the Son of Man would be delivered up into the hands of men who would kill him. But they did not understand and were afraid to ask him' **(Mark 9.30-32.)**

'The soldiers spat upon him' **(Matthew 27.30).** The soldiers spat upon his face, the worst insult inflicted by one person on another. On the Mount Jesus face had been transformed like the sun, but now thus was the sacred face of the Saviour disfigured. *'They took a reed and struck Jesus on the head'* **(Matthew 27.30).** The sacred head crowned with beauty was thus disfigured.

'O sacred head sore wounded
With grief and shame weighed down
How does that visage languish
Which once was bright as morn'

The sacred face of Jesus was distorted with insult and humiliation Pain was etched irrevocably upon that sacred face. Through the circle of thorns, the crown of shame. But it is there in that disfigured face of our Jesus on the cross that we see the saving face of God the Father. Pointing to the crucified Christ, Paul shouted out

'For God who said, 'Let light shine out of darkness, has shone into our hearts to give the light of the knowledge of the glory of God in the face of Jesus Christ' **(2 Corinthians 4.6)**

For true knowledge of God is found and understood only in that sacred but disfigured face of Jesus Christ. One day we will see Jesus the resurrected Lord of our heart and soul, faith and worship 'Jesus' face shone like the sun shining in full strength'.

'Jesus' servants shall worship him and shall see his face'
(Revelation 1 6 and 22 3-4)

One of the Bible's greatest passages is the great Aaronic blessing, uttered over the people by the high priest on the great Day of Atonement.   May this be your blessing

> *'The Lord bless thee and keep thee*
> *The Lord make his face to shine upon thee*
> *and be gracious unto thee*
> *The Lord lift up his countenance upon thee*
> *and give thee peace'* **(Numbers   6.22-26)**

3   THE HEM OF HIS GARMENT

How close do we need to approach Jesus to gain fellowship with our Lord? How many volumes of prayer must be offered up on the altar of worship before the believer can be assured of a personal intimacy with the Saviour? What weight of rigorous spiritual exercises must we carry on our shoulders only to dump at the feet of Christ before we are assured that Jesus has noticed us and is paying any attention to us? One saintly man performed all such tasks but to no avail. He felt so far from the Christ he sought even in the fulfilment of these spiritual exercises.

On 17 July 1505 Martin Luther entered the Augustinian monastery at Erfurt. His aim was to find peace with God, and to escape from the turmoil of his soul. He engaged in every spiritual exercise, followed every prescribed religious path, and even undertook a pilgrimage to Rome. But all to no avail. In Luther's estimation no one could satisfy the demands of the Almighty, nor rise to the standards of Christ the Saviour. He wrote *'I was a good monk and I kept the rule of my order so strictly that I may say that if ever a monk got into heaven by his monkery it was I'* But he was also to admit his own sense of failure and his awareness of personal shortcomings. He wrote in his commentary on 'The Sermon on the Mount' *'This word is too high and too hard that anyone should fulfil it. This is proved not merely by our Lord's word, but by our own experience and feeling'.*

Then how can the believer reach out to gain fellowship with the Lord?   How can the believer know that inner certainty manifesting itself through an even deeper inner peace?

This is a story of an authentic perfect sacramental communion between a few souls and their Christ. My friend was a fine man, an outer radiance shone from a pure soul. His last illness was so severe, preventing the consumption of any food, liquid or solid. There was a danger he would choke. But my dear friend wanted the Sacrament of Communion. This is what we did. With his finger my friend touched the broken bread then touched his mouth. Likewise with his finger he touched the wine in the blessed cup then moistened the outside of his lips. By the touch of a finger the broken bread and blessed cup became for us all a full communion and a perfect sacrament. Christ filled that scene. Much later in my ministry I had occasion to repeat a similar sacrament and the wholesome effect was exactly the same. That slight touch of the finger on bread and wine, then transferred to mouth and lip, was sufficient for Christ to create his own full fellowship.

Believers need not fear that their fellowship is broken and their spiritual exercises are in vain, especially in these seasons when our faith flows at the ebb tide. We can still hear the whisper of his voice. But, on the other hand, Christ will always detect the slightest echo of our prayers. Bishop R H Lightfoot was one of the giants of New Testament studies. In one of his works he rightly points out that in the Gospels we can only hear the whisper of Christ's voice. But that whisper is sometimes all that we require, for it will prove to be sufficient to encourage our faith. On the other hand Christ the Lord will always hear the prayers of the faithful, however faint they may be. Astronomers with their superb instrumentation have discovered so much about our living universe. Nowadays they call our world the multiverse. They have detected in certain areas of space very faint tremors. They call these tremors the cosmic background radiation. They are so faint that a flake of snow falling to the ground will make more noise. They believe that these are the last faint sounds from the singularity we call the Big Bang of 15 billion years ago when our universe came into existence. How much more can Christ the Lord pick up the echo of your prayer even if that prayer is fainter than a snow flake falling to the ground.

A Meditation

'If I can but touch his garment I shall be healed' **(Mark 5.28)**

Lord Jesus, in the press of the crowd, cloak with cloak, garments jostling in the crowd, at the very moment she feared to have lost Christ, her outstretched hand and seeking finger touched the hem of his garment. She was well, and Jesus knew that he had healed her for God's power had gone from him **(Mark 5.30)**.

Lord Jesus,
We yearn for you that the finger of our faith
    might just touch the hem of your garment,
    and our soul might just skim the edge of your presence
That will be sufficient for all our needs.
Just a gentle touch on the outskirts of your presence
    sufficient to heal our faith from the fullness of your saving
    grace.
Our wait has been long, and our pain has been sore
    costly for our faith spent all but to no comfort.
But our faint faith touched the hem of your healing
Lord, the slightest touch from our finger of faith
    the gentlest ripple from your healing grace
    'Tis all we require, from the hem of your garment'.

Lord Jesus
She said, *'Yes, Lord, but even the dogs eat the crumbs that fall from the master's table'* **(Matthew 15.21-28)** Lord Jesus, if we can but eat the very crumbs from the master's table, we will be filled *'Blessed are you when you hunger and thirst after righteousness'* **(Matthew 5.6)** *'For even a crumb of your heavenly bread shall be sufficient for us. Lord Jesus Christ, you are our Bread of Life'* **(John 6.35)**

Gentle God,
In their wilderness journey you gave them manna, food from
    heaven
    *'For they did eat of the bread of angels, for you sent them
    food in abundance'* **(Psalm 78.25)**
In our pilgrimage in life
Jesus gave us not the bread of angels,
    but the bread for sinners

'Jesus took bread, blessed it, broke it.
'This is my body which is broken for you' **(Matthew 26.26)**
Lord Jesus, Host of the Lord's Table
One crumb, one sacramental crumb, is all we need
Yet to us, before wondering eyes, you offer a feast
    'This is my body broken for you'
'Tis all we need
One crumb from the Master's Table

Lord Jesus
If we can but hear the simple whisper of your voice
    then the ear of faith shall listen and the soul be gladdened.
One heavenly syllable, can encompass all our knowledge
    can impart all our wisdom.
For often above, below, within earthquake, wind and fire
    we hear the still, small voice. **(1 Kings 19.11-14)**
    'a low murmuring sound'. (NEB)
For when that whisper invites,
    'Come unto me and I will give you rest' **(Matthew 11.28-30)**
Then, Gentle Jesus,
The whisper of your voice,
    the word of eternal life' **(John 6.68)**
'Tis all we need to hear.

Lord Jesus
Ours is the assurance
That you need only plant the seed of faith within us
As small as a grain of mustard seed
And with that faith we can move mountains **(Matthew 17.20)**
And all our thoughts, joys or sorrows
Can find a resting place in your faith
As the birds of the air find rest in a tree **(Matthew 13.31)**
Jesus
How little you need place within us
    to achieve so much for us.
Your presence is our encouragement,
    we rest in its' nearness. **(Mark 6.31)**
In your absence,

we prepare for your return. **(Matthew 24.45-47)**
The sound of your voice is our guidance,
  but in your silence you still speak to us.
Jesus, One simple gentle touch of your finger
  then we are alive in your faithfulness.
One simple touch
'Tis all we need

4 REASSURANCE

> *'And the stately ships go on*
> *To their haven under the hill*
> *But O for the touch of a vanish'd hand*
> *And the sound of a voice that is still'*
>
> **(Tennyson 'The Brook')**

Tennyson's poetry speaks for everyone who has lost someone near and dear, a husband or wife, brother or sister, a child. Someone bereaving suffers an utter desolation, of such intensity that it can never be described, so immediate it can never be shared. Until it happens no one can know what it is like to be left alone. 'But O for the touch of a vanish'd hand, and the sound of a voice that is still'. The psalmist wrote, *'Yea though I walk through the valley of the shadow of death'* **(Psalm 23.4)** The Hebrew text reads, *'Yea though I walk through the valley of deepest darkness'*

There is a gorge nestling on the northern side of Ben Attow in Wester Ross. It is situated three miles into the hills from the main road, and that walk itself into the hills is breathtaking in more ways than one. The gorge is long, its walls high, the ground underneath is rough. Here the climber finds the first snow of the winter and the last of the spring. The gorge can act like a funnel, the north wind can defy a climber and turn him back from his walk. But when the climber emerges from that gorge the vast sweep of valley and mountain displays a panoramic view of unlimited dimensions.

When we lose someone it is as if we are walking through a deep gorge, *'Yea though I walk through the valley of the shadow of death'.* But when we try to continue our life. It is as if we emerge from the gorge into broad daylight. But we know we have left someone behind in the valley

As the days go by our pain may be eased but shall never go away. Time simply does not heal. We may succeed in carrying our loss, but we shall never fill it. But the day will come when we will look at that photograph once again. In an unguarded moment a gentle image from the past, that loved one's past, will flit before us like a soft breeze in a summer evening, like a wisp of cloud in a quiet day. The tear will swiftly flood the eye and the heart immediately trembles. Then, by God's grace and the inner resolve of mind and will, a simple smile will lighten our face, and a serene memory will gladden our heart. Then we will and we can, in a tangible way feel the touch of that vanished hand, and audibly hear the sound of a voice that is still.

A Meditation

'O death where is your sting, O grave where is your victory'
(1 Corinthians 15.55)
Gentle God
I need not ask these two baleful foes,
I know where they dwell.
The sting of death is my broken heart,
grave's victory is my empty life.
A light went out now all is grey,
the spark of life, now there is none.
Gentle God
Often I am caught unawares,
the silent room waiting my returning steps.
The passing thought, 'I'll need to tell.'.
the chair unused,
The card, the letter, unopened, with their unspoken message
Gentle God
Will there be any release from this unreal world that is all too real?
Can I return to my old self, for my thoughts belong to a stranger within me?
Will I ever know peace? *The peace of God passing all understanding, keeping guard, sentinel watch, over my heart and soul'* **(Philippians 4.7)**
Will I ever lead a normal life, but now what is normal?

Gentle God
> I will walk smartly, but I stumble.
> I will be strong, but inwardly I tremble.
> I will worship, with a soul as silent as an empty cathedral.
> An open prayer book with a closed message.
> A favourite hymn with silenced words.

Gentle God
> Time passes but does not heal,
> people do remember, many forget.
> Life goes on, creeps on,
> 'From day to day till the last syllable of recorded time,
> and all our yesterdays…'

Gentle God
> *'Touch me, as the Living One touched the bier and brought life'* **(Luke 7.14)**
> *Weep with me, as the Living One wept over a grave filled by his friend* **(John. 11.35)**
> Gather me, living God, from the grave of mourning He once occupied.
> Living God, ease within me the death-sting He once endured
> That slowly and with pain
> > I might see the 'rainbow through the rain'
> > > And the horizon of life though with tear-filled eyes.

Gentle God
> With faltering words I will say
> 'O death where is your sting, O grave where is your victory?'
> Then, help me to know, more to believe,
> That beyond that horizon
> *'The Lamb who is in the midst of the throne is feeding my loved one*
> *Does lead my beloved to living fountains of water,*
> *And that God, the Gentle God did wipe away all tears from these eyes'* **(Revelation 7.17)**

As you did from your Son's eyes
As you will from my eyes
> Then, I will feel the touch of a vanished hand
> And hear the sound of a voice that is still'

5 WHEN GOD SPEAKS

'Comfort ye, comfort ye, my people, says your God
Speak tenderly to Jerusalem' **(Isaiah 40.1)**

In 597 BC Nebuchadrezzar captured the city of Jerusalem and ten years later destroyed the city and its temple. In 597, 587, and 582 drove after drove of the people were taken eastwards from Judah in what was later called the Exile, or the Babylonian Captivity. Their towns and villages were evacuated, their fields and farms were left unguarded and were soon occupied by the Samaritans from the north. Their nationhood was destroyed with the fall of their monarchy, Judaism, their unique religion, was virtually destroyed with the demolition of the temple. Incidentally, one book alone from the Hebrew Scriptures helped to preserve Judaism, it was the Book of Psalms.

The major prophets were prominent at this crucial period in the history of Israel. Jeremiah had predicted the collapse of his nation before the disastrous events had occurred. But his warnings fell on deaf ears, *'You proclaim peace, peace, where there is no peace'* **(Jeremiah 8.11).** Ezekiel accompanied his people into the exile.

Ezekiel supported and protected them, and assured his people that God had not abandoned them as they had feared. The destruction of city and temple signalled their demise. But Ezekiel encouraged them to believe that God had not forsaken them. *'For thus says the Lord, I will search for my sheep as a shepherd seeks for his sheep that are scattered'* **(Ezekiel 34.11-12).** The deported people were allowed to settle in Babylon, build houses, live in their own communities, and worship according to their own religion. Many imagined that their God Yahweh had abandoned them and consequently they often adopted the worship of Babylon's foreign gods.

At this critical period the prophecies found in Isaiah 40-55 were given to the Jewish people through the prophet we know as Deutero-Isaiah. The entire book of Isaiah is composed of three parts. The middle section (chapters 40-55) is called Deutero-Isaiah, or Second-Isaiah. This entire section highlights the sovereignty of God, his supreme rule over every nation whom he uses to fulfil his purposes. These chapters declare the uniqueness and holiness of God, in marked contrast to the pagan gods of the other nations. I consider these chapters to be the high water mark in the Hebrew Scriptures (the Old Testament). This section opens with the dramatic words immortalised in Handel's 'Messiah'

'Comfort ye, comfort ye, my people, says your God
Speak tenderly to Jerusalem **(Isaiah 40.1)**

Speak 'tenderly' to Jerusalem. The Hebrew text for 'tenderly' is 'hal leb' and it literally means to speak 'from above the heart' In English when we want to express ourselves in a deep way we speak 'From the bottom of the heart'. In Hebrew the expression is reversed. When God speaks tenderly to his people God speaks from 'above the heart'. It is like the picture of a gentle brazier fire warming God's words for his people before he utters them. When God wants to speak to his people God speaks from the heart.

A Meditation

'Thus says the Lord'
    For God speaks to every generation and to all peoples
But always God speaks from the heart

Thus says the Lord whose word we must obey
    'I am the Lord your God
    who brought you out of the land of Egypt' **(Exodus 20.1)**
You gave us your word,
    to follow and obey that word
    was wholesome life and inner peace.
We broke you word
    before we broke your word we broke your heart, (John Calvin)
    still you spoke to us tenderly from above the heart,
From above your broken heart.

Thus says the Lord to whom we offer praise and prayer
    'Hear O Israel, the Lord your God is one God
    Worship the Lord your God with all your heart and soul and
    life' **(Deuteronomy 6.4)**
Bless us when we worship you,
    but chide us when the devotion of our soul turns cold,
    but even when you chide us,

You speak tenderly from the heart.
Thus says the Lord who remains ever faithful
'My steadfast love shall not depart from you
My covenant of peace shall not be removed
Says the Lord who always has compassion on you' **(Isaiah 54.10)**
By what infinite compassion can you remain faithful to us?
your covenant of peace, have we not destroyed it?
your compassion, do we still deserve it?
Lord, we do not deserve you.
But still you are faithful, speaking tenderly from the heart
Thus says the Lord
But there was a day, a life
When yours was not a spoken word,
But the living Word, even Jesus
Then you did speak most tenderly to your people
'I thank you Father, Lord of heaven and earth
You have revealed these things to the innocent
Such was your gracious will' **(Matthew 11.25-26)**
You speak tenderly to your people in Jesus
Then do we respond.
'O Lord, speak to us, your servants are listening' **(1 Samuel 3.9)**
Speak, O Lord.
Speak tenderly
From above the heart
Then, Gentle God, we will speak to you
with sincere words because you are true
from loyal faith for you are trusting us
in obedient lives for you are controlling us
Then, Gentle God,
As you speak tenderly to us from above the heart,
we will converse with you, tenderly.
'From the bottom of our heart'

6 ONE WORD IN CONCLUSION

Thank you God
For the little things that mean so much
personal moments we treasure.

Unending kindnesses from lovely friends
     gentle words yet strong and gracious.
In quiet moments filled with memories
     we are not alone.
Pensive thoughts shared with no one
     myriads of precious images
     multicoloured scenes in shadow and light.
Many fine people, a cloud of witnesses.
Jesus
From such scenes
You make for us 'Summer Days'

Chapter 5

THE COMPASSION OF CHRIST

"THE SEVEN WORDS FROM THE CROSS"

Dietrich Bonhoeffer will always be remembered for his opposition to Hitler and the National Socialist Movement. Imprisoned during the war years the volume of his 'Letters from Prison' was his defiant expression of commitment to Christ and his defence of the Christian Gospel wherein he paid the full 'cost of discipleship'. Throughout his imprisonment his demeanour influenced both his fellow prisoners and his captors. He spoke for the last time to his fellow prisoners during worship on Sunday 8 April 1945. The next day at Flossenburg he was hanged.

There are countless occasions when someone's words were immortalised by his or her death. On the cross as he died Jesus spoke seven words, etched into human history, written large across the conscience of humankind.

The Compassion of Christ

'Jesus was led to the place where malefactors were usually executed to make his death the more shameful. We should weigh God's purpose more closely. God wished His Son

101

*thrown out of the city, as unfit to share men's society, in order
to take us into the heavenly Kingdom along with the angels.
The more insult and shame He bore in the face of the world,
the more acceptable and noble the spectacle He gave in His
death to God and the angels. The foulness of the place was
no hindrance to His erecting there the glorious triumph of His victory*
(John Calvin)

In that foul place seven pure words were heard,
uttered by the Holy Son of God

We revere them as the Seven Words from the Cross.
In these words we encounter the Compassion of Christ

1   FATHER FORGIVE THEM

'Father forgive them they know not what they do'
(Luke 23.34)

They had been married for over thirty years. Then in one rash act he had an affair. His wife saw their marriage dissolve in betrayal, their home and family reduced to ruins. Explanations failed to ease the sharp pain, while his assurances could not re-build her trust. Healing and renewal could only come from the broken heart of a betrayed wife. Standing in the ruins of her hopes and trust, speaking from the hurt of her sore soul and broken heart, only she, the suffering victim, could say to the one who caused her pain, 'I forgive you'.

We are commanded to forgive one another as God forgives us **(Matthew 6.12)**. Forgiveness heals wounds and reconciles differences. But forgiveness can only come from the victim to the oppressor. We can never expect forgiveness as a matter of course. Nor can we ever say, 'I forgive myself'. Only the person who has been hurt can forgive the other who caused the hurt. We can only 'be forgiven' by someone else. In the deepest way forgiveness comes from God, *'Who can forgive but God alone?'* **(Mark 2.-12 especially verse 7)**. In forgiveness we receive God's 'pardon'.

The word 'pardon' comes from two Latin words 'per donum', 'through a gift'. Forgiveness is God's gift. On the Cross God's forgiveness is full and overflowing. It is God's 'pardon', God's gift of saving grace. Forgiveness must not be confined to the narrow boundaries of belief. Forgiveness encompasses the entire spectrum of personal relationships. Without forgiveness personal reactions can be reduced to vendetta-type tit-for-tat conduct. Forgiveness is the pinnacle of inter-personal behaviour, the supreme response of one person to another. It is the emotional attitude capable of responding to others in the most mature and wholesome manner. As such it reflects God attitude and response to men and women.

'By this word Christ not only remits their punishment. But he commends to God his Father the salvation of the men by whom He was more than cruelly harassed' **(John Calvin)**

A Meditation
'Father forgive them'
We cannot forgive ourselves
    we can only be forgiven.
Only forgiving can heal the wound
    cleanse the stain,
    gather the separated.
Forgiving heals the personal wounds of soul
    the spiritual wounds of spirit.
Forgiving cleanses evil
    and removes the stain of sin.
Forgiving re-unites divided persons,
    self with self, self with others.
Forgiving re-unites the eternally divided
God and man.
They were right to declare but wrong to deny against the Christ
    'Who can forgive but God alone?' **(Mark 2.7)**
Who can even dare to begin to forgive between man and man?
    The Jacob-caused hurt in Esau
    The Cain-spilled blood from Abel's veins
Then who can forgive between God and man?
    the stain of the Judas kiss,
    so deep that the stain on the skin
    becomes the wound in the soul
The soul of the Christ, God-man
    and we are all Judas.

'Who can forgive but God alone?'

The departing back of the denying Peter
>   For we are that Peter.
The thrusting fist of the doubting Thomas
>   and our little faith is the fist of the Thomas within.
>   *'Who can forgive but God alone?'*
>   *'God shows his forgiving love towards us*
>   *that while we were yet sinners Christ died for us'* **(Romans 5.8)**
>   'Father forgive them'

Forgiving comes only from the hurt-ed one.
>   the wounded soul, the broken one
'Father forgive them'
>   the passion of the Crucified One, Son of God,
>   reaches out from pain and darkness
>   to the eternal sorrow of God the Father
God the Father, God the Forgiver
'For who can forgive but God alone'

For if the passion of the crucified Son of God
>   is answered by the eternal sorrow of God the Father
>   whose will is fulfilled in that crucified One
Then, the pleading cry, 'Father forgive them'
>   from the passion of the crucified Son
>   is answered by only the forgiving Father
The inner mystery of God
>   is the passion of the crucified Son
>   being answered by the agony of the crucifying Father
>   in the Spirit uniting will and deed
But the inner heart and soul
Of that inner mystery of the Godhead
The inner mystery within the inner mystery
Is Forgiveness
'Father forgive them'

The conversation between Son and Father in the Spirit
>   speaks of forgiveness
>   when the will of the Father
>   is at-one with the will of the Son

in the bond of the Spirit
This is forgiveness
Forgiving belongs to God.
Love is of God for God is love.
Forgiving is of God for God is forgiveness.
This forgiveness is the eternal certainty of personal salvation.
We are what we are because of forgiveness.
Praise be to God for God's forgiveness.
  Your pardon over us.
  Your free gift of saving grace.

2 PARADISE

'Today you shall be with me in Paradise'
(Luke 23.43)

This is a true story. She was very young to be so ill. Yet she shared with her gentle parents the knowledge that her time was limited. I watched them enter into her pain in such a caring and committed way that they felt for her and with her. I saw her enjoy the wider scope of their healthy days, because they took her with them in love and wholesomeness, so that for brief moments she overcame her restrictions of ill health. Then it was all over. The little bed was dismantled but otherwise the room remained unaltered. It became a simple but peace-filled domestic shrine. They grieved in the same wholesome way in which they had cared. For they knew that after pain had come relief, following distress she has been welcomed by peace and rest – in the Paradise of God. I was a young and inexperienced probationer minister and I learned so much from that family.

'Paradise' is an ancient Iranian word, imported into the Hebrew language. It means a walled garden. In the Old Testament it refers to the original and pristine Garden of Eden, where the first man and woman lived in harmony. In the New Testament Paradise describes the future city of God, with the river of life, and the fruiting trees. The Paradise promised to the criminal on the cross was the place of rest after death.   Jesus still promises these things to us. It would be easy to restrict the idea of Paradise to religious connotations. But the idea of rest after labour and striving properly belongs to the whole life-experience.

'A shining instance of God's grace is seen in the conversion of this man' **(John Calvin)**

A Meditation.

Father God,
>If Christ be not crucified for us
>>then not for us a Paradise of rest
>>>but only the Sheol of distress.

All we like sheep have gone astray
>we are lost, we deserve to be lost.

Saviour Christ, remember us in your kingly glory **(Luke 23.42-3)**

What words are these we hear?
Uttered by the Crucified One, the Desolate,
>crucified with us and for us.

What words are we hearing,
>as we hang with Him on Calvary's hill?
>*'Come unto me and I will give you rest*
>*Take my yoke upon you and learn of me*
>*You will find my yoke easy to bear'*
>*My yoke is rest for your soul'* **(Matthew 11.28-30)**

But I will take your yoke on my shoulders
>and receive it into my heart.

Your yoke is hard to bear
>it is distress and pain for my soul
>*'This day you shall rest with me in Paradise'*
>*'Blessed are those who die in the Lord.*
>*They rest from their labours*
>*and their works do follow them'* **(Revelation 14.13)**

Saviour Lord
We dare not have our works to follow us
>they will chorus a cry of accusation against us.

They will rear themselves as flaming swords barring our way to
>the tree of life and to that first Paradise, that Garden of
>Eden. **(Genesis 3.24).**

Saviour Lord
You took the burden of our life with you
'He descended into hell'
You left it there
'The third day He rose again from the dead'
Then our works will not follow us,
    nor our sins condemn
    'They were given a white robe,
    and rest for a while until the completed time' **(Revelation 6.11)**
Saviour Lord
A white robe!
    ours are the tattered rags of sinfulness,
    the soiled garments of broken lives.
But they took his seamless robe and would not tear it
    rather for it they cast lots **(John 19.23-24)**
If we can but touch the hem of that seamless robe
    then we shall not go naked in our rags and tattered
    garments.
What is this with which you clothe us, that seamless robe?
    'Tis white, pure and clean.
        Miracle of saving love that robe makes us like itself
            pure and clean
Saviour Lord
No, do not wear our rags
    nor clothe yourself with our sinful garments.
Yet you do,
This is what you have done

    'This day you shall rest with me in Paradise'
    'To him who conquers I will grant to eat of the tree of life
    which is in the paradise of God' **(Revelation 2.7).**
    'You shall eat of all trees except the tree of
    the knowledge of good and evil'
    'The day you eat of the tree from that tree you shall be
    barred from the Eden Garden, the Paradise of God.
    Then you shall not eat of the tree of life' **(Genesis 2.16-17).**
Father God
Wretched knowledge we gained when we disobeyed you,
    bitter fruit on the tree of the knowledge of good and evil.

Naked we stand before you
> with no garment of beauty to cover our shame.

Lead us heavenly Father
> who walked in the Garden in the cool of the day

Lead us that we might eat of the tree of life.
Tasting the fruits of saving grace and forgiving mercy,
> for the tree of life
>> was the cross of death
>>> was cross-shaped for the Saviour

'Today you shall be with me at rest in Paradise'
'I know a man in Christ who was caught up into Paradise
and he heard things that cannot be told' **(2 Corinthians 12. 1-4)**

Saviour Lord
When that day comes, gather us unto yourself in your paradise
> *'Remember us in your kingly glory'* (Luke 23.43)

Then we will hear words beyond our ability to repeat,
> we shall see beauty, the very reflection of God's glory,
>> we shall be our self, our true self - discovered in God.

We shall see you, Saviour Lord
> *'Not as through a glass darkly, but face to face'.*
> **(1 Corinthians 13.12)**

Because
> the *'spirit and glory of the Lord shall rest upon us'* **(1 Peter 4.14).**
> *'In the Paradise of God'* **(Revelation 2.7).**

3   JESUS' FAMILY

'Woman behold thy son, son behold thy mother'
(John 19.25-27)

I wished her a 'Merry Christmas' and asked her if she would be with family for the New Year. She was a lovely lady, but her lack of words and little speaking suggested a deeper secret in the soul. My cheerful words fell silent. 'How can I have a Merry Christmas?   It was on Christmas Day during the war when my husband's ship was torpedoed and he was lost at sea. The following New Year my only son was killed in action. I have no family to celebrate New Year. The family home can and should be the safest and most intimate place on earth. Our home – a little piece of heaven planted on earth.

The ancient tradition details how John the beloved disciple cared for Mary the mother of Jesus. John probably took Mary to Ephesus. Archaeological ruins still bear their names. Jesus had been misunderstood by his family **(Mark 3. 31-35).** But from his very birth Mary the mother of Jesus pondered many things in her heart **(Luke 2.33-35 & 2.51).** Now she stood at the foot of the cross, her son's cross. She understood everything. Theologians are often guilty of distorting the Christian message, or making complicated what is so straightforward. This accusation can be made against the church's theological teaching and doctrine of Mary the mother of Jesus. The excessive Mariology development in the Roman Catholic Church is balanced by the narrow-minded bias in the Protestant Church concerning Mary the mother of Jesus. If only all Christians would stand at the foot of the cross and hear our crucified Lord speaking to his heart-broken mother. This domestic scene from the most unlikely place, the foot of the cross, highlights in such a positive way the place and importance of home and family.

'Yet, if we consider the details of time and place, Christ's dutifulness towards his mother was wonderful. I pass over the extreme tortures to His body. I pass over the reproaches. And although frightful blasphemies against God exhausted his mind with incredible sorrow, and although he sustained a dreadful contest against eternal death and the devil, none of this prevented His solicitude for His mother'.
(John Calvin)

A   Meditation

-to lead us through the progressive stages of Mary's life

'My soul doth magnify the Lord
and my spirit doth rejoice in God my Saviour' **(Luke 1.46-47).**
'See that broken figure at the foot of the cross, her son's cross'
There was a youth-filled day when that young virgin maiden
    was the handmaid of the Lord.
    for she bore the divine Son, the Christ
'You shall call him 'Jesus',
    he comes to save his people'. **(Matthew 1.21)**
Mary the one person to whom the Spirit came,

into a home and within a family
'(and a sword shall pierce through your own soul also)'

'See that broken figure at the foot of the cross, her son's cross'.
    They brought for his purification the turtledoves and pigeons,
    but they brought for our purification the One to be the,
    'Lamb of God who takes away the sins of the world' **(John 1.29)**
    Even then did a sword pierce a mother's soul **(Luke 2.35).**
    that soul was a mother in a home and family

    'His mother kept all these things in her heart' **(Luke 2.51).**
'See that broken figure at the foot of a cross, her son's cross'
    'Son how you have treated your father and mother so badly!'
    'How ?, I must treat my heavenly Father so obediently!'
    'Son, come home with us!'
    'But I am at home in my Father's house!' **(Luke 2.41-50).**
Mary pondered these things in her heart
    Who was this child
        she had to call JESUS?
    Often in the daily routine of a Nazareth home
        she shivered
    'A sword in her heart'

'Is not this the carpenter, the son of Mary' **(Mark 6.3)**
'See that broken figure at the foot of the cross, her son's cross"
Did they doubt Mary when they could not understand her son?
    did a mother fall foul of the petty comment,
    the ignorant talk, the little minds.
Hurtful words but all the more piercing in her pain,
    in one so sensitive and pure, the handmaiden of the Lord?

    'His mother and brothers came and called for him.
    They said, your mother and brothers are outside asking for you'
    He replied, 'Who are my mother and brothers?'
    'The ones who do the will of God' **(Mark 3.31-34).**
'See that broken figure at the foot of the cross, her son's cross'.
He was son in the home, first born from her womb,
    yet at times apart, almost a stranger.

'I must be about my Father's business'
Mary pondered in a pierced heart
for a sword shall pierce her soul

Did that mother joyfully see the healed man, the restored child, the happy home where gladness was reborn? Was this the Father's business? But why does that mother harbour that fear, a fear to pierce the heart? That sword whose cold shaft was ever felt, whose sharp strike was ever feared. Was that lonely mother in that crowd when they cast palm branches below his feet and their garments in front of his approaching steps?

'Hosanna in the highest
Blessed is he who comes in the name of the Lord' **(Mark 11.8-10).**

BLESSED

'Blessed?'
Is this the blessing of the Lord?
'Behold your king is coming to you
Humble mounted on an ass' **(Zechariah 9.9 and Matthew 21.5).**

How she came to be at that cross she cannot remember
she dare not look up
'See that broken figure at the foot of the cross, her son's cross'
Images flash before tear-filled eyes
Bethlehem and Nazareth, a quiet home by the Sea of Galilee
'Blessed are the poor in spirit' **(Matthew 5.3)**
The neighbours told her they had never heard such preaching **(Matthew 7.28)**

The gentle knock on the door when the widow of Nain came to thank her **(Luke 7.11)** Jairus' wife and her little daughter **(Mark 5.41)** The father of the epileptic son now cured and smiling.**(Mark 9.27)**. The clean skinned smile of the restored leper **(Mark 1.40)**

A thousand images in a flash
A voice broke into her world
'Woman behold thy son
Son behold thy mother'
'See that broken figure at the foot of the cross, her son's cross'.

111

4 MY GOD, MY GOD, WHY HAST THOU FORSAKEN ME?'
(Psalm 22.1 and Matthew 27.46)

He was a God-fearing man and a regular worshipper.His son was lost at sea, and that loss brought his wife to an early grave. All within the space of twelve short months. He was a fine fisherman and could handle that fishing boat in the worst of all weathers. Yet he never fished again. As we left the cemetery on the second visit in that fateful year he said to me, 'This is my Gethsemane'. Then, he added, 'Now I know what the Lord meant when he said, 'My God why hast thou forsaken me?"

These words brought light to Martin Luther, and continue to do so for many distressed souls.   In 1511 Luther was teaching in the university of Wittenberg. He was very distressed, finding no comfort for his troubled soul in the spiritual exercises of the church. He had to lecture on the Book of Psalms. He reached Psalm 22 and Jesus' lonely cry of utter godforsakenness. Our Lord's plea is the loneliest cry ever from the human soul. This was the eternal price God paid for us, the complete sacrifice given for us. The loneliness of Gethsemane **(Matthew 26.36-46)** is deepened to unimaginable levels of desolation which we cannot fully comprehend. We can only bow in utter helplessness and humility before the awful weight in these words. This was Christ's 'unbearable burden' **(Karl Barth).**

'There appeared to be more than human vigour in Christ's cry, but it is certain that intensity of grief forced it from Him. This was His chief conflict, harder than any other agony that in His anguish He was not given relief by His Father's aid or favour, but made to feel somehow estranged. He did not merely offer His body as the price of our reconciliation with God, but also in His soul He bore our due pains. When the trial came on Jesus in this form, He was now against God and doomed to ruin' **(John Calvin)**

A Meditation

'Eli, Eli, lama sabachthani'
'Godforsakenness'
      the last experience for God and people
         beyond which there is nothing

because the nothingness has already been
encountered
in the godforsakeness
the last, ultimate experience of
annihilation.

But godforsakenness exists
experienced by people
ultimately experienced by God.

Because in godforsakenness
God turns his back upon the soul,
closes his heart,
forgets the soul ever existed,
It is ultimate
God turns his back upon himself,
closes his own heart to his own love,
somehow God forgets himself.

Godforsakenness,
the spiritual black hole
No one can enter therein
BUT ONE DID
No one can survive
BUT ONE DID
No one can re-emerge from its bourn
BUT ONE DID

One called JESUS
'Eli, Eli lama sabachthani'
'My God, my God, why hast thou forsaken me?'
Jesus entered
The black hole of the soul,
soul's blackness curving light back into darkness,
spiritual anti-matter destroying life in nothingness.
Anti-Christ
Anti-God denying God
but denying God within God.
Jesus entered
'and preached to the spirits in prison' **(1 Peter 3.19)**

'My God, my God why hast thou forsaken me?'
in the darkness Jesus saw them.
from their lifeless state Jesus raised them from the dead.
despite their nothingness Jesus renewed them.
Whom did he see?
to whom did he give life?
in whom did he renew the soul?
'Twas to the spirits in prison to whom he preached'
Jesus did these things to you and I
for we are these spirits in prison.
for we were there,
to us he came
God did these things for us
In his life in Jesus
What words gave us, life-less souls, a new life?
what did he preach to release us from that prison?
The strong man's house **(Mark 3.27).**
Jesus said
'If anyone will follow me let them deny themselves
in self-forsakenness.
'Take up their cross
in God-given renewal.
Then follow me **(Mark 8.34-37).**
Jesus asks us
'How can a soul be regained from nothingness
once it is lost into nothingness?
Only by sacrificing self
into the self-sacrifice of God.
Only by giving one's self
into the self-giving of Jesus.
Only by forsaking one's self
and fleeing into the Godforsaken One.
Who cried
'Eli, Eli, lama sabachthani?'

5 'I THIRST'
(John 19.28)
Doctors, priests and ministers among other professions devote their

lives to caring for people. I always considered it a privilege that I could visit homes and families and they would take me into their trust and share their experiences with me. Often I visited them in hospital after they had undergone serious surgery, or when a loved one was near to dying. A nurse would regularly moisten dried lips and a parched mouth with a little cold water. That small amount of water was sufficient to give respite to the sick and dying. *'A little drop of water in Christ's name' will not pass unrewarded* **(Matthew 10.42).** Jesus said, 'I thirst'.

It was custom that when a condemned man was suffering the extreme and final agonies of his crucifixion that a sponge soaked in drugs was administered to him to deaden his pain. This lethal drink was often administered to the wretched man by the gentry ladies of that time **(Matthew 27.48. Mark 15.36 Luke 23.36, John 19.29).** At first Jesus refused their drinks. But John Calvin pointed out that Jesus only took the sponge at the very point of death, when his work of salvation was completed and his sacrifice fulfilled. Jesus promised a blessing to those who hungered and thirsted after righteousness **(Matthew 5.6).** Jesus promises us his life as *'a well of water springing up to eternal life'* **(John 4.13-15).** But at his end, Jesus thirsted, the well of life ceased to flow within him. Empty in body and soul, Jesus had given us everything.

'Christ does not ask for drink until all things have been accomplished; and thus he testifies his infinite love or us and his inestimable care for our salvation. No words can fully express what bitter sorrows he endured; and yet he does nor desire to be free from them until he has satisfied the justice of God' **(John Calvin)**

A Meditation

Heavenly Father
Our Lord's Holy steps walked this earth and with their imprint
    'the thirsty ground became springs of water' **(Isaiah 35.7).**
Yet at the end when all was accomplished Christ did thirst
Smiting hard against stubborn rock the Moses rod brought
    water from the broken stone **(Numbers 20.11)**
But smitten harder by the rods of evil men

the submissive Saviour cried out from a broken body,
'If anyone thirsts let him come to me' **(John 7.37)**
But you must come to me here where I am to be found
Waiting for you – on this cross
    The Crucified One is waiting for you.
Seek the Saviour where he is to be found on that cross,
    call upon him there, on that cross
where he comes near to you' **(See Isaiah 55. 1-6).**
Yet at the end the Giver of the water of life could only say
    'I thirst'
The Blessing One promised to bless those
    'who hunger and thirst after righteousness' **(Matthew 5.6)**
Yet the Blessing One wanted for a blessing.
Without a blessing the Blessed One
    became the Accursed One – condemned.
Therefore did He thirst
For, Blessed One, the blessing you yearned to receive
    was our coming to you.
How often we did not seek the Lord where he was to be found,
    nor call upon you when you were near to us.
On that cross
How often we did not listen when you cried in your
    cross-shaped agony
'Ho everyone who thirsts come to the water, the water of life
    we sought instead the broken cisterns.
Therefore did you thirst

Heavenly Father
    'Like as an hart pants after the water brooks
    So thirsts our soul after you, O God' **(Psalm 42.1-3)**
We need to return to you, O God.
    We need to hear the voice of Him who promises
I will give you, I will be unto you.
    'The spring and fountainhead, the well of water,
    surging within you to eternal life' **(John 4.15).**
For only when we come to you shall we cease to hunger,
    only when we trust you shall we never thirst,
        but we can only come to you where you did thirst.

On that cross
  Our forefather gave us this well to drink from.
But, heavenly Father, on that cross,
    you have given us the fountainhead,
    the spring of eternal life

I THIRST
A Meditation

Heavenly Father
The Saviour Christ did thirst, accomplished all 'It is finished'
Then
    We shall hunger no more, neither thirst anymore
    For the Lamb who is in the midst of the throne that shall
    feed us
    Shall lead us to living fountains of water
    God shall wipe away all tears from our eyes
    In like manner as God first dried the tears from his holy Son
    (Revelation 7.17).

6 'IT IS FINISHED'

(John 19.30)

After forty years as a minister one would think that I would be totally at ease with every duty for a clergyman. Yet one duty confronts me with a challenge which has remained undiminished over the decades. That duty is the conduct of a funeral service. One gentle minister chided his colleagues for taking funeral services then hurrying away to the next piece of work. We should pause a little for something absolute has happened, a life has departed from our ken. For us in this temporal scene there is an awesome finality in the dying of a loved one. How much more does the death of Jesus add an overwhelming weight to his words, 'It is finished'.

John 17 has been called Jesus' 'High Priestly Prayer'. Uttered by Jesus on the night he was betrayed. In this great prayer Jesus offered his life to God his Father in total   surrender. *'Father my hour has come, I have glorified you on earth, I have accomplished the work you gave me to do'* **(John 17.1-6)**

The Greek word for finished is 'teleo' which means to finish, complete, or fulfil. Jesus' life was not abruptly ended on the cross, rather it was 'fulfilled'. That is the awesomeness of Calvary and the Empty Tomb. Easter with the death and resurrection of our Lord is the completion of Christ saving life and the fulfilment of God the Father's salvific purpose. For this purpose was Jesus born. The incarnation, the birth of Jesus, reaches out to Easter, to Christ's death and resurrection. While Easter, the passion of our Lord, is the fulfilment of Christ's holy birth and life. In the same vein the holy ministry of our Lord was not a preliminary interlude, a preamble to prepare the believer for the epic Easter events. Rather our Lord's holy ministry must be viewed under the shadow cast by the cross standing before the radiant light of the resurrection. Christ's teaching and acts were saving words and deeds.

'Now this word of Christ is most memorable, for it teaches us that the whole accomplishing of our salvation and all the parts of it are contained in his death'
(John Calvin)

A Meditation
'It is finished'
> the whole accomplishing of our salvation
> and no parts are missing
The will of the Father – fulfilled
In the work of the Son – completed
By the willingness of the Spirit
For the welfare of mortal people – accomplished

'It is finished'
> The will of the Father is fulfilled
> The Father *'who destined us, all mortals, in love to be his children'*
> *having chosen mortals in the Son before the very*
> *foundations were laid'* **(Ephesians 1.3-4)**

The will of God
> To be God for and unto people, men women children
The will of God
> To be Father unto mortals he wished to call His children
The will of God
> Older than the foundations on which we stand

Companion with the love of God
Both from the very heart of God
    So of the heart and soul of God
Thus, in that very time-caught moment
        In these mortal words
        'IT IS FINISHED'
For the willing God, loving God
        Living God
        All is accomplished, all is finished

'It is Finished'
        The work of the Son is completed
They told us of his Coming
        That bright Star, these heavenly hosts.
        'For the Star came to rest where the Child was' **(Matthew 2.9).**
        'Suddenly there was with the angel
        a multitude of the heavenly host' **(Luke 2.13).**
They left our sight
        but continued to watch over the Holy One of God
That same Star smiled over the healed leper
        the dead son of a widowed mother
And when to the poor the good news was preached
        The heavenly host shouted out again
            'Glory to God in the highest and on earth peace and
            goodwill'
For peace was brought to the earth
And goodwill created among people
        By the Holy One of God
            Glory be to God in the highest
For 'twas the work of the Son being done
        but not yet fulfilled

'It is Finished'
        But why does this Star shine pale?
            Why are the voices of that heavenly choir so silent?
The Holy Son of God looked in vain for a light,
        a heavenly Star in that Garden.
And He sought in vain to hear even an echo, a soft note,
        from that heavenly choir who welcomed his Birth

but would be silent at his death
'Father if it is possible let this cup pass from before me'
(Mark 14.36).
Father if it is possible let me see but a glimpse of that Star
And hear but a simple sound from that heavenly choir
To know that you are with me
'But not my will but yours be done' **(Mark 14.36).**
'That I might fulfil the work thou hast given me to do'
(John 17.4).
But no light shone
No music was heard

'It is Finished'
'It was about the sixth hour
There was darkness over the whole land until the ninth hour
And the sun's light failed' **(Luke 23.44-45).**
'IT IS FINSIHED
HE BOWED HIS HEAD
AND GAVE UP HIS SPIRIT'

'It is Finished'
O Star of Bethlehem
you stopped over that manger rude
you stooped low with gentle light over that crude manger
smiling at the Holy Child
Now, Star of Bethlehem
stoop low once more
over the crude grave of the Holy One of God
an unwelcoming resting place,
The Bethlehem of dying
but your stellar countenance carries no smile
for our evening rain showers are but your tears
'It is Finished',
O heavenly choir
gladly you did sing to fill the heavens with your happy chorus
over the Bethlehem of the Holy Child
Sing not your praises
but find a gentle lament

and sing a hushed song of mourning
'Glory to God in the highest' you did sing
But God's glory is veiled in a shroud
And low lies his Son.
The Holy One of God
His work is accomplished

'It is Finished'
The will of the Father fulfilled in the work of the Son
The work of the Son accomplished by the will of the Father
Within the life-breath of the Spirit
'And Jesus gave up his spirit' **(John 19.30).**
Jesus gave up his spirit, soul, and life-breath
Jesus released his spirit unto God
The soul of the Father receive the spirit of the Son
The life-breath of the dying Son, released, into the
Life-breath of the living Father
The life of the Son
One in living
Now one in dying
In the life of the Father
In the life-breath of the Spirit

'It is Finished'
And all for mortal creatures
For the welfare of frail people
'Crucify him', we had shouted
'They know not what they say' He had replied

7   FATHER, INTO THY HANDS I COMMEND MY SPIRIT'
(Psalm 31.5 and Luke 23.46)

He was a great shepherd and a skilled gillie, and he knew his hills and glens. But he was a torment to follow on these hills as his long paced strides covered the rough terrain with ease and left us hill climbers in his wake. We thought we were fit on the hills until we walked their slopes by his side, or soon behind his steps. He was admitted to hospital, little was said in the family home or within the Highland community where he had spent his days. For everyone both knew and accepted his condition. I visited him in that ward so far removed from the glens where we used to meet. A young minister I stammered broken words about 'the end' feeling it my duty to broach the subject. He sensed the drift of my thought and propped himself on the bed. 'Tom', he said, 'I thatched my house when the weather was fine, and I am ready to meet my Maker'.

The last words spoken by Jesus on the cross are the opening lines from Psalm 31. 'Father into thy hands I commit my spirit. These words have been a source of deep comfort to many greats souls in their last hours. Martin Luther was one such saint. In the utter faithfulness of God his Father Jesus Christ is safe and liberated. We, too, are safe and set free in the love of God our Father, flowing into us through Jesus' compassion. In his last moment, that hour of deepest darkness, Jesus commits himself to God the Father in the deepest act of trust. God is for Jesus the one who redeems, God the Father is the faithful God.

'There could be no clearer declaration of triumph than for Christ to boast without fear that God is the faithful Guardian of His soul. He (Christ) took His words direct to God and entrusted His testimony of confidence into His very bosom. He wished His words to be heard by men, but even if it did no good in men's sight, He was content if God were His only witness'

'Now let us remember that it was not for His personal interest that Christ commended His soul to the Father, but he gathered up, as it were, all the souls of his faithful in one bundle, to keep them safe with his own' **(John Calvin)**

A Meditation

The psalmist said
> O, God,
> *'My spirit I commit into your hand*
> *For faithful is your heart, Redeemer God'* **(Psalm 31.5)**

So said our Saviour Christ to his God and Father
> 'My spirit I commit into your hands'
> > for these holy hands are secure
> My spirit I commit into your heart
> > for faithful is the heart of God, my God

Redeemer God
   'You have been our dwelling place in all generations
   From everlasting to everlasting you are God' **(Psalm 90.1-2).**
The Redeemer God
   'I know that my redeemer lives' **(Job 19.25).**
   'The eternal God is our refuge
   And underneath us are the everlasting arms'
   (Deuteronomy 33.27).
May we ask of you, Saviour Christ
   by your spear-pierced side let us walk
   in your nail-pierced footsteps let us follow
Into you nail-pierced hands we commit our lives
And at our ending
Gather our soul into your bundle of life
   that it may be safe with your own.
May we say eternal God, Redeemer God
   When our time touches eternity's time
   And our years are gathered into God's timelessness
      'Into Your hands I commit my spirit'
      Listen to my last cry
 as You harkened unto Christ's.
      Be my faithful God
         as You were to Christ.

'Joseph of Arimathea came and took away Jesus' body,
Also, Nicodemus who had first come to Jesus at night.
Now in the place where Jesus was crucified there was a garden,
and in the garden a new tomb, where no one had ever been laid.
They laid Jesus there.'
(St. John's Gospel 19.38-42)

Lamb of God who takes away the sins of the world
Have mercy upon us
Lamb of God who takes away the sins of the world
Have mercy upon us
Lamb of God who takes away the sins of the world
Grant us your peace
('The Agnus Dei')

Chapter 6

PAISLEY CHRISTIAN SOCIAL ACTION CENTRE

I had followed him over the waste piece of ground in the west end of Paisley towards the darkened and derelict houses. We reached the old tower shaped outside staircase and ascended the stairs. They were wedge shaped like pieces of cheese, and I stumbled to keep my feet on the broken steps. He had gone ahead of me, familiar with this derelict building even in the dark, he easily reached the top of the stair case and quickly plunged through the opening in the wall where once a door had hung. I succeeded in cracking my head a few times as I went through the gaping holes in the wall.

We were now in the bedroom of what had been at one time a nice house. She lay in the corner. The fireplace was filled with the ash of burnt newspapers, their only   source of heating. The glassless window was hopelessly covered by a sheet of corrugated iron that flapped in the night wind offering no protection from the creeping cold air. I cannot remember their names, but their memory will live with me to the grave. They were homeless, they were two lovely people, and I still admire them. We had only recently opened the Christian Action Centre for overnight accommodation. We were able to house only the men folk, because there were far more of them, and because we did not have the resources to build facilities for both sexes. At first he had accepted a bed in the Centre, glad to spend the night under cover.

Then he dramatically left, and surrendered his place to another man.

He hid himself away, but after some time I did find him. This was his story. When he came into the Centre's overnight accommodation he had been going about with his woman companion. The relationship was wholesome; he acted as her male protector. Had she been alone then there was a moral danger that she might be attacked. For him to come into the Centre at night placed her at risk. So he surrendered his place at the Centre in order to be with her in that dark and dismal derelict building.

I had had to persuade him over a few weeks to let me come and see where they lived. I stood in the darkness and my heart went out to them. That night, back home in the warmth and comfort of the manse I wept through my evening prayers. Because in that derelict room I had seen Another Person, I had seen Jesus crouched against the wall shielding himself from the cold. I had left him there with my two friends.

'Foxes have holes and the birds of the air have nests
But the Son of Man has nowhere to lay his head' **(Matthew 8.20)**

True Advent

For nearly twenty years the Paisley Christian Social Action Centre flourished in Paisley. It began as a refuge for homeless men and women, but developed into a highly efficient rehabilitation Centre where homeless people were given the chance to regain their place in society. A few ministers within the former Paisley Presbytery had become aware of the growing number of homeless men and women in Renfrewshire. Unable to pass by on the other side any longer they arrived at the idea of using a derelict church building to help the homeless. The inspiration and leadership from this band of clergymen demonstrated the ministry of the church at its finest. I count myself privileged to be numbered among them.

In the 18th Century three churches had been build by the government of the day to care for the spiritual needs of the people of Paisley, a town now expanding in size and population through the thread industry. The first of these churches was built at the foot of New Street, so they called it the Laigh, or Low church. The second

126

church was built at the top of the same hill so, following good Scottish logic, they called this second one the High Church. The third church was finally built half way up the hill, and again with sound reasoning they called it the Middle Church. It was to this third church, the Middle Church, that these ministers turned their attention.

Advent 1975 was an exhilarating demonstration of what the Christian community could achieve. We had eventually succeeded in making some space in the derelict church suitable for day use. We served hot breakfasts, distributed clothing and at the start, were able to provide a few hours of shelter for the homeless men and women. Our opening breakfast session occurred during the first week of Advent 1975. A few weeks earlier we had held a meeting to which anyone from the churches, interested in helping us, was invited. Many wonderful Christians attended our meeting, heard our plans, and promptly told us to go and get on with it and they would support us

Support us they certainly did. We drew up a rota of teams from the local churches   to make the hot breakfast, serve and tidy up afterwards. We worked under the most appalling conditions, for this building was in a wretched state of disrepair. Often we had to sweep the water from the corridor floors before we could begin in the morning. The poorly repaired roof could not resist the fierce winter storms. These helpers   came at 7 o'clock every morning in all weathers to prepare the food. This pattern of rota teams lasted for nearly fifteen years. It was a wonderful example of true Christianity, real faith, dedicated service. It was accomplished with genuine care and kindness for the homeless men and women but in the strength and name of Jesus Christ. Words cannot describe the genuine Christian service performed over these years by Christ-loving Christians from every denomination of the church. These duties were carried out cheerfully and lovingly.

That first Advent was memorable. The teachers in the Home Economics department in my chaplaincy school knitted scarves and gloves. They made and sold tablet and with the money we bought socks and other items of warm clothing. Members from the many churches now becoming actively involved in the Centre also raised money   through a wide variety of means and efforts. We ministers were becoming versatile at begging. We went round the local bakery shops, there were a few local shops at that time, and their owners promised us their help. So, Christmas morning 1975 became very special. We were able to provide our friends with a hot breakfast. We were able to give them useful gifts of warm woollen clothes. And through the generosity of the bakers and others, we were able to give them a parcel of food for the rest of the day, cigarettes and the like, but no alcohol. We felt very humble as we tidied up the Centre that morning. We did not feel proud or superior, only humbled. But something else took place that morning with the gentle power to break us. As we tidied the kitchen we heard our homeless friends singing 'Still the Night, Holy the Night'. They were not good singers, but their rendition brought us to tears.

Sleeping Rough

Before we opened our facilities in the Middle Church we had gone round the several locations in Paisley where we knew men and women were sleeping rough.

At the outset we organised a rota of helpers who distributed soup and bread. A derelict building was a favourite but dangerous place. One favourite area was the arches underneath the main railway line. I used to visit these arches. One night a chap, high on something, made a lunge at me. I went back the next night, but he was not there. At the very back of the arches an untidy heap of old clothing would suddenly turn. It was someone's bed. There was a human being under that pile of filthy material. The basic policy was simple and straightforward. We provided food last thing at night, then breakfast in the morning. We hoped that the 'skippers' as they were called would survive the winter weather. Many did not make it. In the first three years of our operations three homeless per year succumbed to the bad weather, ill health, and abused living. In some of these cases we were the ones who conducted the funeral services.

After we had opened the Centre the need for the late night soup run continued. There were too few places in the Centre for those needing accommodation. So I continued the soup run. The normal meeting place was the Tunnel. This was the basic servicing area for the office blocks and shopping precincts in the centre of Paisley. This was a favourite place because the ventilation shafts from the heating systems from the buildings regularly gushed out their hot air. The skippers stood around the openings from these air ducts and gained a modicum of warmth during the cold nights.

One night they were all huddled together on a cement ramp. As I prepared the soup and sandwiches on the level ground I asked them why they were clustered together. 'Because there is a rat running about and its right behind you now' was their reply.

Often these men would disappear. This was a danger signal. Perhaps they had taken ill, were hurt or injured in a fight or overdosed. I went looking for one of the regular chaps. It was a bright winter night with a full moon. I had been told that my friend, for they were my friends, had been last seen at one particular spot. I went through the old gate into the backyard of derelict buildings facing on to the main street. Underfoot the ground was covered with hundreds of empty beer cans and bottles making walking conditions hazardous. I went forward through another break in the wall. Suddenly a cat jumped out behind me with a real din from the cans and bottles. But it might as well have been a homeless man, high on meth or some other potion burning him up. I could have lain there for long enough, nobody knew where I was. God be my judge, my instant alarm was immediately followed by a deep sense of protection. The same Jesus whom I had left behind in the derelict building was there beside me. My son never went to sleep until he heard the front door close behind his returning father.

Our Friends

For in a breathtakingly short time they had become our friends. They began to trust us, and we heard human stories for they were men and women. They had lived well until that traumatic event changed their lives forever. They had held positions of responsibility. Now they could not trust themselves with a penny. They had let themselves go down, and nobody had been there to stop them fall nor arrest their decline into misery. We became their friends, and we valued these friends as equals. We tried to be to them what Christ was to us.

Overnight Accommodation

The pressing need for overnight accommodation was now overwhelming. We were distressed at having to evict these homeless men and women from the Centre in mid morning after their breakfast. They were irritated that they were not allowed to remain within the building. With the professional help and personal encouragement of two fine Christian architects plans were designed and applications submitted to local authorities. The result was the creation of two dormitories collectively housing about twenty men. We had reached our goal at last. For the next three winters in the early 1980's the streets of Paisley and Renfrewshire were free from men and women sleeping rough. Somehow the women folk were able to get a bed for the night from transient friends. Nobody remained outside at night.

Now we could begin the real work of restoration. Regular food, showering, changes of clothing. A wonderful Christian doctor agreed to be our medical adviser and practitioner for the residents at the Centre. He advised us on things medical from head lice (before it became fashionable again) to the general medical condition of our homeless friends after their many excesses. We encouraged them, with a lot of persuasion, to take a shower before they put on pyjamas, before they went to bed. What was a shower, what do I do with this sachet of hair shampoo? 'You open it and wash your hair'. Showers, nightwear, a clean fresh bed. Surely we had accomplished something right and proper.

'A larger pair of shoes?' 'Yes, I need a larger pair of shoes'. From the abundant store of clean good quality used clothing we were giving a clean pair of socks to the residents every morning. Dutifully they were taken and put on. Until after ten days one of the residents came with the strange request, 'I need a bigger pair of shoes'. For ten days he had been putting on the fresh pair of socks on top of all the others. Little wonder he needed a large fitting shoe!

'Can I get a better coat, this one if fraying at the cuffs?' I looked at my friend   dressed in what had been a very expensive overcoat. Suddenly that simple request opened a new vision for us. Something had happened to our friend, and to the other residents. He was not being fussy in asking for a better coat. Rather he was beginning to take a pride in himself. Now he was feeling a sense of responsibility for his own appearance, no longer content to walk the streets in shabby clothing. Needless to say our friend got a better coat. We stopped receiving and distributing second hand clothing, and made strenuous efforts to raise the funds to buy new clothes for the men.

But human nature can be very hard. It is made of what Immanuel Kant described as 'the twisted timber of humanity'. He was not a nice resident, he was always drunk and aggressive. One night in the toilet under the influence, he fell. In the fall he banged his head and he died. The police surgeon reported that the fall he sustained could have contributed to his death. The family tried to sue us for lack of care. For six months we lived as if on Death Row. It was as if the family of the man who fell among thieves sued the Good Samaritan for further injuries to their relative due to the uneven passage on the donkey en route to the inn **(Luke 10)**.

The Rehabilitation Programme

'Can I get a better coat, this one is frayed at the sleeves?' This simple request triggered a whole raft of ideas and aims, silently maturing in our hearts and minds. It was not sufficient to feed and clothe these friends. For if it is true that 'man shall not live by bread alone' then it is also true that there is more to life than the food we eat and the clothes we wear. *'Consider the lilies of the field and the birds of the air'* **(Matthew 6)**. To restore to them true human experiences, to help them regain a sense of personal worth, to teach and support them so that they could be responsible for their own personal lives, to regain self respect, a sense of dignity, these had to be the ultimate aims and achievements for the Christian Action Centre.

They were unable to cook and prepare meals. They could not cope with money, and budget their Social Security money for the full length of a week. They did not know what to shop for, how to prepare a cheap but wholesome meal. For these were the real and practical steps they had to take in order to be restored to society, in order for them to realise their full potential as human beings.

So, we opened a new section in the Middle Church, this time a great advancement and improvement from the dormitory accommodation. There were four separate bed-sit rooms for the residents whose improved life style showed that they could regain their place in society. These four bed-sit rooms opened into a common living room. The latter had basic cooking facilities. The residents in this new apartment had their own room, for which they were responsible. They could prepare their own breakfast and lunch, they ate their main meal in the dining room area. Most importantly, when we went to see them in their own accommodation, we did not simply knock and enter. Rather, we knocked on the door of their own residence, then waited for the men to invite us in.

A volunteer support helper was assigned to each of the four residents. These were not professional care workers. Rather, they were church members who had the skill and knowledge to teach and help the residents. Supremely they also had the love of Jesus in their lives. They brought that added dimension to their supportive caring role. Their task lay in helping the residents in their own personal domestic and home care. They showed them how to budget their money to make it last throughout the week, how to shop, what to buy, how to make a good wholesome meal out of very little. In other words all that a mother, a wife, a housekeeper takes for granted were taught to our residents.

The Wide World

We now had a fully developed programme for rehabilitation. This programme followed three distinctive stages. The first stage was the reception of these homeless people. This included regularising their daily timetable, the provision of good food at regular meal times, instilling in them the need for proper personal hygiene, proper clothing, day activities and proper sleep at night. Medical examination to see they were all right in health and strength. The second stage in our rehabilitation programme involved a gradual but real shift from our total governance over their lives to one where they assumed a greater degree of control over and responsibility for their lives. To this end we constructed a separate part in the Middle Church. Here there was a common living room area, from which four single rooms were set out. Each man had his own room for which he was personally responsible. He kept it clean, neat and tidy, was responsible for his bed and personal clothing. The single common room had simple facilities for cooking, where the men prepared their own breakfasts and lunches, while having their main meal of the day with the others. They were also responsible for the use of their own weekly money. They were supported and guided by a one-to-one Christian carer who helped with cleaning, organising their food purchasing, and the budgeting of their money so that a week's money lasted for a week. The third stage in this rehabilitation programme saw these men move out into their own flats in the community. Since they were unable, or ineligible to secure a tenancy of their own a unique plan was drawn up. The renting agency, at that time the District Council, rented flats to the Board of the Christian Action Centre. We were corporate tenants in these flats. We in turn gave them to the men who paid us for the rent but who otherwise enjoyed the full tenancy. Again when the men left the Centre to return to the community there was a two-fold support system in place. First they were assured clearly and lovingly that they could return for a visit to see us at any time. Secondly we seconded one of our Christian helpers to continue caring for the men by regular visits in their new homes just to see that things were still all right.

Christian Caring

The entire rehabilitation programme was inspired by and based upon the Christian form of service and caring. Christian caring and service drove our whole impetus. At every stage we saw ourselves as servants to these men. Never did we allow ourselves to be regarded as superior to, or in charge over the men. We always regarded ourselves merely as Christ's 'douloi', menial servants, for the sake of these men **(2 Corinthians 4.5).**

Our programme differed in stark contrast from that employed by the secular local authorities. Their politically driven policy of offering council housing accommodation to everyone including the homeless 'skippers' was in my opinion doomed from the start. It was simply not good enough to give a homeless person the key to a council house and let that person get on with it. A long period of time was often required to stabilise and teach a homeless person the necessary personal and domestic skills required for acceptable residence in the community.

A Derelict Building

It had now become obvious to me that radical changes were required in the management of the Centre to meet the developing situation and to broaden the involvement of a wider community in our work. First of all we were still an unlimited company. Had anything gone wrong that required a large expenditure then the members of the Board would have been personally responsible for finding major funds. In other words we were financially responsible. So I started to draw up a new constitution to make the Centre a company limited by guarantee. But the other major development that could have taken place was the broadening of the management structure. By this time, with years of reliable service behind us the Centre was a recognised caring organisation, recognised by the District and Regional authorities, generously supported by the community at large, respected by the public at large, and supported by and involving all the denominations of the Christian Church. A golden opportunity presented itself to establish a Board that represented   statutory bodies, the churches, and individuals from the community. It would have been a wonderful chance for statutory authorities and charities, for professionals and amateurs, for people from every walk of life to co-operate in what might well have become a centre of excellence and a prototype for caring for the homeless.

The Achilles Heel

It was not to be. When I presented my proposal to establish a Limited Company the local Presbytery took this opportunity to wrest full control of the Centre from my grasp and establish its own overriding control over the operation of the Centre. My vision disappeared like a dream.

Aftermath

The dream that was the Christian Action Centre disappeared. But the memories accumulated over these years will survive in the hearts of many wonderful Christians. For my part I cherish the deepest love and the highest respect for the countless Christians from every denomination who took part in the work of the Paisley Christian Social Action Centre. In particular my fellow Christians with whom I worked in close contact in the management of the Centre. Everyone showed a truly Christ-like witness through countless deeds and endless hours of service.

Postscript

During the last two years of my ministry before my retirement in 2004 I met a young man whose mother had been at the Centre in the very early years. He too was homeless, and he too, had a young woman companion whom he protected. Memories returned of that bleak winter night, the fireplace filled with burnt newspapers, the cold and damp. They were staying in a derelict shed behind a public house in the very centre of Paisley. They could not gain entrance to the new homeless Centre. It was too up market for their wretched state. So during that winter I was once again taking soup, sandwiches, and clothing to the homeless.

The pattern was repeated the following winter when I found more skippers. They were sleeping underneath the roof area of the car park at Renfrew District Offices, at the entrance opposite the great Paisley Abbey. They reminded me of the marginalized whom Gandhi used to meet. They moved through the shadows of the night, disappeared with the coming of day, and the good folks of Paisley went about their business and did not know these people ever existed.

Jesus was right, and still is, *'The poor you have with you always'.* But he also warned, *"I was hungry and you gave me no food, I was thirsty and you gave me no drink, I was a stranger and you did not welcome me in, I was naked and you did not clothe me, I was sick and you did not visit me. …… Truly, I say to you as you did not do it to one of the least of these my brethren you did not do it unto me"* **(Matthew 25. 31-40).**   For it is how society deals with the poor, reacts to them, and cares for them that in the end really matters. As I said in my closing address to Greenock and Paisley Presbytery the challenge of the homeless remains with us. Has the Christian community, and society at large, risen to that challenge? I do not think so.

Gratitude

I look back on these years of the Christian Action Centre with great happiness and excitement. For a brief period the Christian community as a whole erupted into an uncontrolled movement of freedom wherein many homeless people found help and care, love and strength. I hold the many wonderful people who served, witnessed and loved in the Centre close to my heart with deep gratitude to God our Gentle Father through Jesus the Friend of the lost and outcast.

Chapter 7

THE FAR COUNTRY

The Parable of the Prodigal Son
(Luke 15.11-32)

PART 1 INTRODUCTION

1   Pictures

This parable story of the Prodigal Son tells the whole Gospel story. It has inspired artists like Rembrandt, to compose their paintings, and theologians to create thoughtful writings. But this particular parable, in keeping with all the parables, reaches out to excite and attract a vast circle of believers. It can be said with justification that the parable of the Prodigal Son narrates the Gospel story.   Moreover with this parable we can paint different pictures of human life and experience. We can identify with their characters, for they create scenes with which we are familiar. The parable tells a story similar to our own life journey, which is often our 'way into the Far Country'. We embarked on our life journey of discovery.   Our days were young, the world waiting to be conquered.   Often we stumbled and fell, on many occasions success was accompanied by loss.   Now perhaps the colours of life have become grey like the hairs of an aged head.

Our life experience can be that Far Country to which the prodigal son travelled. We have journeyed through the passing years of our life as sojourners in our own far country.

2   St. Luke's Gospel

The Good News for Outsiders

Over the centuries on stained glass windows, in illustrated manuscripts, in carefully structured books, the four Gospels have been depicted by symbols. The symbol for Luke's Gospel is a calf, the animal of sacrifice. Among the four Gospels Luke's account shows most clearly how Jesus broke down barriers, bringing salvation to everyone. In Luke we see Jesus reaching out to embrace everyone, Jew and Gentile, slave and free the greatest and the least. The three 'lost and found' parables of the sheep, the wedding coin and the prodigal son are Luke's response to the criticism levelled against Jesus for mixing with what one commentator called the 'near-nobodies' of society. 'Now the tax gatherers and sinners were all drawing near to Jesus. The Pharisees and scribes murmured, *'This man receives sinners and eats with them'* **(Luke 15.1-2).** This is God's salvation found in Jesus. But Jesus only accomplished God's will and salvation through sacrifice.

3   The Accomplished Work of God

Jesus' birth life and ministry, passion and rising, is God's salvation. God's salvation is with us here and now. God's salvation is not shaped by the events of history. But rather by its presence in the world, God's salvation directs the course of history and controls the forces of our destiny. Jesus' living presence is both the promise of God and its very fulfilment. God's finished salvation in Christ has created an entirely new life, a life radically different from human greed and wrong. God's new life of salvation is not an alternative option for people to choose or set aside at will. Rather it is the new life of the kingdom confronting people with God's offer and humanity's choice. God has established his kingdom of saving grace within the realms of human experience. God has placed salvation within reach of human hands, planting it within the recesses of the human heart and soul. The Gospel is God's invitation to enter that kingdom of redeeming love, to be renewed in that saving life, and thereby to become the true and genuine human being we were created to be. Luke's Gospel is unique in the way it extends an invitation to everyone to enter the realm of God's kingdom of salvation and experience the joy and happiness of salvation.

4   The Outsider

Only someone such as Luke *'the beloved physician'* (**Colossians 4.10**) was able to appreciate this universal outreach of God to embrace everyone in his redeeming love. For Luke was the outsider who came into the predominantly Jewish-Christian community. His two-volume 'Gospel of Luke-Acts of the Apostles' is the only material in the New Testament written by a non-Jew. In all likelihood he was a gentile God-fearer who had associated himself to a local synagogue, and it may well have been the preaching of Paul that won him over to Christ and generated a close personal friendship with Paul himself. Perhaps we can allow our imagination the freedom to think that Paul' preaching may have won over this thoughtful doctor to Jesus.

5   The Universal Gospel

Luke's Gospel has been described as the finest account of the life of Christ ever written and it certainly contains many attractive features. Luke recounts personal details seen by the doctor's practised eye and recorded in his medical notes. Simon's mother-in-law suffered from a 'high fever'. Contemporary medical terminology described fevers as high or low according to their severity (**Luke 4.38-39**).   One outstanding quality featured in Luke's Gospel is the unobstructed openness of Jesus to everyone irrespective of race, social position, or personal history. Simeon's prediction tells that Jesus will be the light for all the nations (**Luke 2.29-32**). The mission of the Twelve to the Jewish people is followed by the mission of the Seventy to the other nations (**Luke 10.1-12**). The significant role given to the Samaritan race in the parable of the Good Samaritan (**Luke 10.. 29-37**) clearly shows Luke's Gospel as a Gospel for all.

PART 2   THE PARABLE OF THE PRODIGAL SON

1   The Prodigal Son

'There was a man who had two sons. The younger one said, 'Father give me the share of property that falls to me. Not many days later the younger son gathered everything he had and took his journey into a far country' (**Luke 15.11 ff**)

Nowhere is that divine invitation extended to us with such clarity of meaning, God-yearning depth of feeling, and magnetic attraction for our faith, than in the parable of the Prodigal Son. Luke's Gospel contains a unique group of parables which do not appear in the other three Gospels. The parable of the Good Samaritan **(Luke 10.25-37)** and the three great 'Lost and Found' parables **(Luke 15)** among which the parable of the Prodigal Son stands foremost. Rightly it has been described as the greatest short story ever written. Henri Nouwen correctly asserts that the whole gospel is contained in this parable.

The parable of the Prodigal Son guided Henri Nouwen, that brilliant yet enigmatic Dutch priest, in his quest for his spiritual home. But another great Dutchman, the painter Rembrandt van Rijn, created an artistic masterpiece which now hangs in the Hermitage State Museum in St.Petersburg. While the great Swiss theologian Karl Barth developed the parable of the Prodigal Son into a deep and thoughtful account of Jesus in 'The Way of the Son of God into the Far Country'

Note

I have written short stories to highlight the many lessons of this parable. They stand independently and are not to be seen as a related narrative. If these narratives help to draw out the depth of this wonderful parable I will be satisfied.

2   The Far Country

He had repeatedly tried to explain to his elder brother that he had not meant to take his share of the family possessions and go off to have a good time. He knew he had failed to make his brother change his mind. But a chance remark from his elder brother made him realise he no longer had any place on the farm.

He had been home for seven months. But seven days ago their father had been gathered to his rest. He had reached the borders of that Further Country and crossed over to be received by Abraham. They had not spoken much, these two brothers sharing the same family, but entirely different in every way. They had met   late one evening by the farm door. The little hill that marked the farm's border was clearly outlined in the evening sky.

'See the little hill, I always beat you in the race to the top'.

His brother stiffened. He smiled, his brother did not like to be beaten or teased.

'There's another world beyond that little hill
There's a Far Country
Have you ever been to the Far Country?'

'Do you know what it is like being the younger of two sons in the family?'
'Of course we would have an equal share of the farm, the house, the property'. 'But remember, you are and will always be the first born son, with the right of the first born'.
'I wanted to make a career for myself, have a life of my own'
'But it was in a strange land, a far country.'

'Have you ever been to a far country and lived with strangers? I had to get to know them, make some contacts, so that I could ply my trade as a joiner. I spent a lot of money meeting people. They seemed friendly enough, promised me some work, there were big contracts in the pipeline. I got some work, but not a great deal. Then the recession hit the building trade, work dried up, they gave what little there   was to their friends. None to me. By this time my money was finished. That's when the trouble started, and I went downhill'.

The two brothers roused themselves from their silent reveries, stiff with their cramped sitting and from the morning chill. In the first light of dawn the outline of the little hill became visible. He reached for trusty staff, prepared to start the unbroken and unchanged routine of yet another day first the cattle then the milking. His younger brother watched him go, a sad smile lining his face. The young man quietly rose, gathered his few belongings, and passed through the yard. He looked for the last time at the new handle he had fashioned for the plough, for he had not lost the carpenter's skill taught to him by his father. He had repaired the dilapidated farm buildings during these last seven months. He breasted the little hill before   journeying once again into the Far Country. That night he found lodgings in a town called Nazareth, and stayed in Joseph's home. There he met another carpenter.

3   'Have you been to the Far Country?'

The Younger Son asks us all.
       'Have you been to the Far Country?'

'Have you been to the Far Country, with cities and many people?
Only to feel alone
Where no-one cares who you are or how you are
Because they are only interested in themselves
Sometimes you find friends, only if you share with them what little you have
You feel you can trust them, only to discover they will betray you
Then leave you alone?'

'Have you been to the Far Country?
And turned ill.
Hungry in body, tormented by pain
Filled with fear.
Pain! You think you are dead
You wish you were
Fear! Lurking in the shadows of the mind
Fear of the unknown, 'What is happening to me?'
Fear of the future, 'What will happen to me?'

'Have you been to the Far Country
And lain in the cold field on many a night
The stars your companion?
The blanket of heaven your cover
A stone for your pillow
You stared desolation in the face
There is no Beth-el'

'Have you ever been to the Far Country
Stood on the brink
Fallen into the deep black pit
Despair's cold hands reach to grasp you
Fear embraces you
The present overwhelms you
There will be no to-morrow?'

'Have you been to the Far Country
and yearned for home?
For comforts passed
Familiar sounds, childhood places
Fireside, food, family
Only to fear they are lost forever

142

Only to regret their passing?'

'Have you been to the Far Country
And lost the SHEMA?
'Hear, O Israel, the Lord your God is one God'
Lost the sound of your word of praise
Alive in the eternal Word of blessing
Lost the sound of the Word
And the faith it sustains
Lost the Fatherhood of God
Who loved the Word in His soul
And planted that Word in your heart?'
'Have you been to the Far Country
Wanting to return home
Wondering if you can
How you will be received
Frightened to find out?'

In this way the Younger Son speaks to us
Then asks
How will you return home from the Far Country?

4 Our Far Country

We can reply
'Yes, I have been to the Far Country
I still sojourn there
For I am weak, I am ill beyond cure
I never thought it would happen to me
Was school's Sports Champion.
They said I had a bright future
Then that numbness, couldn't catch a ball
Running was slower,
Running, now I cannot walk
Seems so long ago, but I am still young
Too much life remaining for this chair
They say there might be a cure some day
It will be too late for me'

'Yes I am in my Far Country
Been my dreary home for many years

I am old now, my journey has been long
The Far Country has been a distant horizon.
I wish the Further Country would come soon.
The family have their own lives to live
Cannot always be running after me
Don't get me wrong
They are good to me
Been a lonely journey these past twenty years
Ever since that illness took him away
We had a good home, its quiet now
Nobody can know how lonely it can be
Until you have been in my Far Country

'Yes, we are in the Far Country
It's hard being married with two children nowadays.
We are still together, we will not leave
He's feeling it, he has changed
Strange, he said the same thing about me the other night
Suppose I have changed
There's no one to talk to
They don't want to hear your moans
Maybe I should have stayed like them
Partners and no children
But we did what we were brought up to do
But I don't go to the Church any longer
I'm sick with worry for him in the streets
He's managed so far, but there's a lot of badness
Where can they go that is safe
Seems a long time ago since I was young'

'Yes, we are in our Far Country
We are still there'

'Is there a way home for us
To return home from the Far Country?'
Is there any way home?
How can we sing the Lord's songs in a Strange Land?

Many are dwelling in their own 'far country' and search for a way home. 'Home' will be comfort and rest from the harsh reality of daily life. 'Home' will be a deeper understanding than the 'I'm sorry' words quickly spoken and easily forgotten. The way home will be accompanied by kind people prepared to enter our experience because they are willing to take us into their heart.

5 The Elder Son

'I stayed at home- for I am the First-Born'.

'I stay at home, I have always stayed here'
I am the First-Born.
> *'The Lord said to Moses, 'Consecrate to me all the first-born, whatever is first to open the womb among the people of Israel, both of man and of beast, is mine"* **(Exodus 13.2).**

I was born without a life that I could call my own
  I opened the womb unto life so I belonged to God
My father and mother paid a price to God that they might keep me
  Another child was there that day in the temple **(Luke 2.22-24).**
  He's a carpenter now in Nazareth
  But he has not stayed at home caring for his parents and family
  Now he travels throughout Galilee   Preaching………
I am the First-Born
  I have been told of this all my life of the honour of this position
  Special place at meals and feasts, I lead the family
  A father' special blessing given only once and to the firstborn.
  A larger share in the inheritance   That's a laugh!
  A larger share of the inheritance
  Being gradually eaten away by that waster, my younger brother
  'Give me a loan father to repay my debts'
And how often have I heard that final warning
  'This is the last time, you will get no more. You are wasting my farm'
Then I had to work all the harder on the farm to balance the books.
My younger brother was to me
  As my forefather Jacob was to Esau - a thief!
He wasted the family's possessions, my possessions.
He could not steal my birthright

I will always be the first-born, his elder brother
But he stole my father's special blessing
>Reserved for the firstborn, and given only once
That special blessing, a father's love
>'He has supplanted me these two times
>He took away my birthright,
>And behold now he has taken away my blessing'
>**(Genesis 27.36)**

He has left home before,
>but not like my forefather Jacob with a mother's blessing
>**(Genesis 37.43-45).**
Because he broke her heart and brought her to an early grave
He deprived me of a mother
He denied me the one who was to be my wife
>Her family would not allow her into our notorious family
Now there are only two of us
For brother has gone for good, I wonder
>For the old man does nothing all day but stare to the distant road
>Hoping he'll return.

But I must work on
>I've never been beyond that little hill
Except to the market
I have a few friends who know my plight and encourage me
>'Come to our place to-night, we are having a party'
But I have always to decline. There is still so much to do

And when I return home
>'What news from the market'
But he is not interested in the good price I gained for the sheep
>Or the orders I received for our fruit because of its high quality
All he meant was simply
>'Has anyone at the market heard anything about your younger
>brother?'
He is away from home, yet his memory broods over this place
>I can never get rid of his curse
I speak to father about the friends I have met at the market,
>'They are having a night out'

But never once did he say
    'Why don't you bring them over here?
    That kid in the field, kill it and have your friends over.
    You need a break'
Never once

Now he has returned
    And I am expected to be happy, to join in the fun

I am remembered as the stubborn son who refused to join in the fun
When my pleasure-seeking brother arrived back home
Yes I was resentful at his treatment that day
Every day when I returned home I have to prepare the meal.
Little chance that I would get time to have a meal with 'my' friends

But there was another reason that day
    Something most people overlook
I had been in the fields all day
I was simply too tired, dusty, and thirsty
I just need a rest to get my breath back
That is, before I made the evening meal
    Not that it was difficult that day
    They had all had a good feed with the fatted calf
    When I saw it and everything else
    I, sort of, didn't feel hungry
    I just had something to drink and I ate after the evening's work
I always have the cattle to bed down for the night
    Sometimes I am out all night,
    Especially if I have the sheep in the fold at the lambing season
    I just curl up in the doorway to the fold
    The sheep cannot escape, the wild cats don't get in **(John 10.1-9).**

Why do I have to do all the work, even the domestic chores?
    Because my mother is dead
    He was her favourite, just like Jacob and Rebekah
    But when he left the house he broke her heart
Now there are only the two of us
    Don't get me wrong. I admire my father.
    He built up this farm, he gave me a chance in life and I
    appreciate that.

Now he is unable to do much about the house
We get on well together. We have a routine. He does what he can.

It is true I have sacrificed a lot for my family
But I don't mind
But it does get lonely at times
You see all your friends enjoying themselves
But you've just to get on with it

I had a girl friend once
There were two sisters, Martha and Mary
Mary was a dreamer. Martha kept the house going
Everyone said that we were well matched
But then she had her old mother to look after
I always thought He was a bit hard on her **(Luke 10.40)**.
We never did get the chance to set up a home of our own'.

There are countless thousands of dedicated family members who have sacrificed their own life to look after aged or sick relatives. There are a disturbingly high number of young children who care for invalided parents, or siblings, often running the house, and continuing with great difficulty to attend school. We dare not forget the selfless people whose unseen, and unrecognised, work brings comfort and kindness to others.

6   The Return of the Prodigal Son

The great painting of the 'Return of the Prodigal Son' hangs in the Hermitage State Museum in St. Petersburg. This masterpiece was painted in the late 1660's by Rembrandt van Rijn (1606-69). The picture shows the elder son staring indifferently into space, unable to accept the return of his younger brother, unwilling to enter into the joy of his old father for this returning beggar son. The picture's centre piece, actually set to one side of the canvas, shows the returning prodigal, on his knees before his father his head resting on his father's lower body. In tatters, his broken shoes allow his bare feet to be torn, cut and bruised by the rough road. He rests his weary head in his father's embrace. But the central figure is the aged but forgiving father. The cloak round his stooped shoulders gently rests on his returning son. His arms embrace the prodigal around his shoulders, so that the lad cannot escape. The dimmed eyes, that grew tired every day scanning the distant horizon are looking at his son, and yet are looking beyond the lad with a faraway gaze. When I saw the original in the Hermitage Museum I went right up to the canvas so that I could look up straight into the father's eyes. The look depicted by Rembrandt indicated that the old father was seeing another horizon, one over which he would soon travel. But his life was complete, he had found his son, his family was re-united and his life's work was accomplished.

7   A Picture of God the Father

Parable or painting the story of the Prodigal Son tells us everything we need to know about God. Or rather, through his Son, God teaches us everything we need to know of God. To be taught by God of God means that we learn about our eternal home and our spiritual homecoming. If the parable of the Prodigal Son inspired Rembrandt, and emboldened theologians like Nouwen, then it was also the fertile soil in which Karl Barth planted the seeds of his theology. In his epic 'Church Dogmatics'. Barth tells the story of the third son, the one who followed the prodigal into the Far Country. Barth speaks of 'The Journey of the Son of God into the Far Country'. This is the truth of the Gospel. When Jesus Christ was born into our human life as a person it was the Son of God who came from the presence of God the Father into our life. The birth of Christ, the Christmas incarnation, is the journey of the Son of God into the Far Country. Christ made that journey to find the lost children of God, to heal them, and to redeem them.

But Barth emphasises the enormous theological truth that when Jesus Christ came to us to heal, liberate and save, then God the Father was with his Son, was in his Son. Or to alter the message of the original parable when the third son volunteered to go look for his brother in the Far Country his old father elected to accompany him. "God Himself came into this world in His Son and as one of us a guest this world of ours He trod" **(Karl Barth)**.

'I will go and look for my brother, I will find him'
The gentle voice of his other son broke into the old man's silence
'Now I will only have one son left, and he is in the fields as always, never any time for me. Increase the grain crop, he wants to pull down

the old barns and build bigger ones. Does he not realise there's more to life, all he wants is increased production. One day his soul will be required of him'.

'Go my son find him, but come back to me, lest I return to my grave with the grief of my forefather Jacob in my heart when beloved Joseph did not return.'

With his father's embrace on his shoulders, and his blessing in his soul, he left to find a brother.

He travelled far. But no one knew of a lost brother, nor cared. No one seemed interested in his story. Often he travelled all day and into the night, and only sought his rest in the open skies, with a stone for his pillow, long after the birds had returned home to their nests and the foxes to their lair. Sometimes to avoid the burden and heat of the day he travelled by night. He soon understood the movement of the stars, and the crescent or waning moon was often his guide. One night he smiled, then burst out in uncontrolled laughter for this particular star seemed brighter, and appeared to move in its own direction as if following a different heavenly movement. That night he followed it, and got lost. The following days and nights were hard to bear. Storm and tempest blotted out his nocturnal friends, cold and ill he felt far from home.

'Go find my son, but come back to me, for you are my Joseph'

Only the echo of these fatherly words gave him the resolve to continue.

He had been travelling for hours and the night darkness had enveloped him. Suddenly in the break of the clouds his star re-appeared. It did shine more brightly, and it did move in obedience to its own command. He hurried on, for in the dawning light even its brightness began to fade. But before it surrendered to the light of day he saw that his star had stopped. It had stopped over a rundown farm. It was dirty in every way so unlike the farm at home. The animals were free to roam wherever they wanted. The only sign of life was a wretched slave chasing after the dirty swine to herd them into an unfenced field and feed them with pods and swill.

He caught his breath. For even in his pitiful rags, beneath the grime and dirt, he recognised his brother.

'Brother, I've come to find you and take you home to father'

Standing in the mud beside his brother, his words made the young lad freeze, before he collapsed in a heap

'Look at me, why have you come, to see my disgrace, to gloat over me.

Will you go home and tell our elder brother what you saw? I know what he'll say, 'He always was a waster''

'No, I have come to take you home to father, he wants you'

'Like this?'

'Yes, just as you are'

They had hardly gone a few steps when a loud and rough voice stopped them in their tracks.

'Where are you going with that slave?'

The dirty unshaven farmer stood over them

'I'm taking him home to his father'

The gentle voice of his brother replied.

''Not before he pays his debts, he owes me a lot for his keep'

'I have no money. I have used it all in my journey. But I promise to send it to you with interest when I return home'

'I've heard that before, as soon as you go over that little hill there I'll never see you again'

That little hill. How often the prodigal had looked at it and remembered the little hill on the outskirts of the farm back home.

'If he goes, you stay'

This was the farmer's last word

'Go, go home to father, he is waiting for you. I will stay here'

'Go, go. Here put these clothes on'.

And with that his brother surrendered his warm garments to the shivering lad.

His head reeling with the welter of mixed emotions the young prodigal found himself leaving the field that reached the little hill. As he climbed over its crest on the way home he looked back. He saw with eyes full of tears his gentle brother putting on his rags, and lifting the pail of pig food to feed the swine.

That is what Jesus did for us when he went into the Far Country to find us and bring us home to God. He stood in our place, was disgraced by the rags of our sin, and paid the price for our debt. That is the Way of the Son of God into the Far Country to find the lost children of God. Christ went with the Father's blessing, but how did the father accompany him there?

8   The Father's Journey

'The hour is coming, indeed has come, when you will leave me alone; yet I am not alone, for the Father is with me' **(John 16.32)**

But where can we possibly see the invisible and eternal God travelling into the Far Country to encounter and find, to live in and be with, creaturely humanity in all our sinfulness and brokenness? In the gospels we see how the Father travelled with the Son into the Far Country.

'They brought a paralytic man carried by four men... Unable to enter the room they opened the roof and lowered the pallet... Jesus saw their faith and said to the paralysed man, 'My son your sins are forgiven' ... Why does this man Jesus speak thus, it is blasphemy! Who can forgive sins but God alone?' Jesus replied, 'Which is it easier to say ..?' 'I say to you, take up your pallet and go home'
(Mark 2.1-12 for the full version)

For the Father was there in the Son, and as the Father gave all things to the Son, so Jesus healed by the power of forgiveness. The Father travelled into the Far Country. 'I am not alone, the Father is with me'

A Meditation

Gentle God,

> In Jesus your Son you travelled into the Far Country of
> > human lostness
> You dwelt with us and your heart was broken and
> > overflowing with pity
> > for our creatureliness
> By the finger of God your Son did break the power of evil
> And establish the kingdom of God **(Luke 11.20)**
> But your healing and saving hands were soil-ed with our
> > sinfulness

'I am not alone the Father is with me'

Gentle God,
>In Jesus you travelled into the Far Country to speak to us.
>The language from the Word of God for our understanding.
>Speech from the Word of God for our saving and healing.
>Healing created in forgiveness.
>>Forgiveness alive in healing.
>Healing born in God's saving soul.
>>Salvation alive in God's healing Son.

'I am not alone, the Father is with me'

Gentle God
>In Jesus you travelled into the Far Country to heal us
>>Lord Jesus, God was with you.
>When you touched the leper to his cleansing.
>>In your speaking to the child in her reviving.
>>>In your blessing of the blind unto their seeing.

'I am not alone the Father is with me'

Gentle God
>In Jesus you travelled into the Far Country to save us.
>>You were in the Garden of Gethsemane,
>>and were frightened.
>You were smitten with the rods for our infirmity.
>>Your head was crowned with thorns.
>Did you don the rags of the prodigal son and feed the
>>swine?

'I am not alone the Father was with me'

Then, Gentle God
>In Jesus you travelled into the Far Country to save us
>Were you with your Son on that Cross?

'I am not alone for the Father is with me'
>Were you with your Son in that Tomb?

'I am not alone, the Father is with me'
>Did you, God, rise again in your Son by the life of God?'
>God unto God

'I am not alone, the Father is with me'

Gentle and Eternal God
>In Jesus you did travel into the Far Country..

You did sojourn among men and women in their
    creatureliness
    and corruption
You did save us through the passion of the cross
You did renew us in the victory of the rising again
Jesus was not alone the Father was with him

O God, you did travel into the Far Country
Gentle God
    How could you feel such love for us
    How deep the suffering in the Godhead
    How infinite the yearning in the soul of the Father
    The more keenly felt because you are pure
    The more gently offered because you are caring
    The more passionately embraced because you are holy
    All for us, frail creatures
    Broken before you,
    What shall we say?

9   The Return Journey Home
'The Homecoming of the Son' of Man'

'Therefore it is said, 'When he ascended on high he led a host of captives, and he gave gifts to men' **(Ephesians 4.8).**
'Thou didst ascend the high mount. Leading captives in thy train, and receiving gifts from men, even among the rebellious, that the Lord God may dwell there' **(Psalm 68.18).**

For Jesus there is the journey of the Son of God into the Far Country to find the lost children. But for Jesus there is the return journey the Homecoming of the Son of Man, bringing God's lost children home to God. But in Jesus it was God Himself who travelled into the Far Country to seek and to save those who were lost. And it was God Himself who returned from the Far Country bearing his children on His shoulders. *'Rejoice with me for I have found the sheep that was lost'* **(Luke 15.6).**
'For thus saith the Lord God, Behold I myself will search for my sheep and will seek them out' **(Ezekiel 34.11).**

One of the central themes in the Old Testament is the utter conviction, the absolute certainty, that the God of Israel would guard and protect his people like a shepherd guiding his sheep. This conviction is expressed in the simple yet profound verses of Psalm 23. God rescued and liberated Israel from the bondage of Egypt and guided his unruly people through the wilderness journey to the Promised Land. During the period of, and in the immediate aftermath of the Babylonian Captivity, the Exile (588-538 BC) the prophets of the Exile spoke of God seeking and finding the lost people of Israel, like a shepherd seeking his lost sheep. *'I will say to the north, Give up, and to the south, Do not withhold. Bring my sons from afar and my daughters from the ends of the earth'* **(Isaiah 43. 1-7).**

But the clearest and fullest developed picture of God restoring his children and returning them home is found in Ezekiel, the prophet of the Exile. *'Thus saith the Lord, 'Behold I myself will search for my sheep. As a shepherd seeks out his flock'* **(Ezekiel 34. 11-31).**

This major Old Testament theme is incorporated into the New Testament's account of how Jesus accomplished God' salvation. Jesus describes his saving ministry as the shepherd seeking the one lost sheep until he finds it, with the ninety and nine safe in the fold **(Luke 15.3-7).** But the clearest self-description from Jesus is found in the Ego Eimi saying, *'I am the Good Shepherd'* **(John 10.11).** The Good Shepherd is also the wounded shepherd who lays down his life for his sheep. This idea of the Good Shepherd is closely associated with the theme of the lamb. Based on the thought of the Passover lamb **(Exodus 12).** John the Baptist declares that Jesus is *'The Lamb of God that takes away the sins of the world'* **(John 1.29).** Finally Jesus died on the Day of Preparation when the Passover lambs were being killed in preparation for the Day of Passover.**(John 19.31)**

Every one of these Biblical ideas weaves a tapestry in rich colours and noble designs. They depict the life and passion of Jesus our Lord, and declare the will and purpose of God for the salvation of the human race. God's salvation is found in Jesus Christ, the Son of God and our Saviour. To conclude our meditation on the Far Country, let us think of the 'Return of the Son of Man from the Far Country, the return home to God the Father.

'Go, go home to father, he is waiting for you'

The gentle brother encouraged the young prodigal as the latter awkwardly struggled into his brother's better clothes. The prodigal's last glimpse of his gentle brother was his fine form bedecked in his own awful rags. For his sake it was better for the returning lad that he did not see what happened next. The gentle brother turned with a warm smile to the dirty rough farmer. Whatever he had wanted to say remained mute, arrested by the vicious blow from the ugly man across the face of the gentle stranger who had taken the place of his former servant.

'He was wounded for our transgressions
and bruised for our iniquities' **(Isaiah 53.5).**

'That'll teach you who is boss around here.' 'You better work harder than that other fellow or you will get more of this'.

The days that followed were even worse. The brute farmer called him mockingly the 'shepherd boy' because he always watched that the sheep were safe at night. There was a fox on the prowl. One night the gentle shepherd surprised the fox which scuttled off to his lair. *'Go home wild fox, you have a place to sleep. But I do not have a place to rest my head'* **(Matthew 8.20)** 'Shepherd boy' the farmer's insult was his comfort, 'David my forefather was once a shepherd boy' The treatment he suffered became more ferocious as the weeks and months elapsed. He tended the sheep especially at lambing time. He encouraged himself with the scriptures of the great prophet *'He will feed his flock like a shepherd, gather the lambs in his arms and gently lead those who are with young'* **(Isaiah 40.11)**

His treatment grew worse. The more he did the more severely was he beaten. It was as if the farmer felt threatened by the stranger who only responded with kindness, grace and love **(Matthew 5.43-48).** He searched his memory for a scripture passage to comfort his weary soul and give him the stamina to continue. Disturbingly the only verse he could remember made him shiver *'All we like sheep have gone astray, and the Lord has laid on him the iniquity of us all'* **(Isaiah 53.6)**

'He is not here, he has gone'

The younger brother spun on his heels, surprised by the quiet voice of the stranger, who was indeed no stranger to him. He had left the family farm, his elder brother was now in complete control. He had decided to come and look for his gentle brother. The speaker was well dressed, and had the appearance of someone enjoying his life. **(Colossians 3.12-15)**   But his rough hands and the evident scars betrayed the fact that he had once been a slave. The younger brother was looking round the farm, his former slave farm. It was neat and clean, the fences repaired, the animals grazing in well kept   fields. Even as he looked the stranger spoke once again,

'Don't you recognise me'

There was something in the speaker's voice that stirred a dim memory.

'Yes, I'm your slave friend from the next farm' 'Remember us all, we are all here, but now we are free'

With that a group of men and women appeared from the outhouses and farm buildings. They surrounded the younger brother, took him into their home, and provided him with food and shelter.

After he had rested the younger brother anxiously pressed his questions.

'But where did my brother go?' 'And what about the old farmer, what happened to him?'

'Your second question is easy to answer', the stranger replied. 'Your brother suffered terribly at the hands of that cruel man' 'But he never once retaliated'

'Like as a lamb led to the slaughter, so he opened not his mouth' **(Isaiah 53.7)**

So a brother thought of a brother as he listened to the speaker.

'Then one day the old man was gone'

'We all said that the old devil was destroyed by your brother's love'

'And we are free, overnight we were set free', they all shouted.

'But where is my brother now?'.

His anxious question nearly choked him. He feared that he would find him buried in a shallow grave, or lost in the rough neighbouring countryside.

'Don't be alarmed, he knew you would return to look for him, and he has left a message for you' *'You are to follow after him'.* **(Mark 16.11)** 'You will be able to keep tracks on his journey' 'Because you will find places like this one where people like us have been set free and given the chance of a new and better life'. 'Wherever you find people like us then you will know that your brother has gone before you'. Then the younger brother remembered what the joiner had said in the house of Joseph of Nazareth.

'I am the Good Shepherd, I call my own, and go before them, leading them out' **(John 10.3).**

The next morning he left the farm of his former shame and slavery. He said a fond farewell to his friends, now like himself free and restored to a proper status in life. His journey continued from one place to the other, and always he found signs in men and women of his Brother's redeeming presence.

In this way Jesus Christ the Son of Man came home to God, and is still coming home to God. This was the Homecoming of the Son of Man to God. As he journeyed from day to day, from place to place, so the Son of Man sets people free. The Son of Man journeys on, from nation to nation, through one succeeding generation to another, from one century into the next. Jesus Christ the Son of Man is still engaged in that homeward journey, still liberating, redeeming, healing, saving, and calling people as he passes. And in his wake generation after generation journey behind him. They travel their way of life as through a wilderness pilgrimage. Their eyes are fixed upon that horizon where space and eternity, time and infinite, merge as one. Theirs is the Promised Land they call the Kingdom of God.

'When he ascended on high he led a host of captives giving the gift of new life to people' **(Ephesians 4.8)**

Chapter 8

A PILGRIMAGE JOURNEY TO EASTER

They were executed before the entire camp these six Jews, one of them a young boy. This was the punishment of Auschwitz. They were hanged. But because he was a little boy and was not heavy, he did not die immediately, but struggled against the tightening rope around his neck. One bystander among the prisoners asked,
'Where is God?' Another replied, 'He is with that little boy'.

What he replied was true, but only half the truth. God was indeed in that little boy as he was in the five adults who died more quickly. But was God also in the hangman, seeing either a soul bereft of feeling or a soul in utter anguish at what he was obliged to do? Was God in the soldiers standing guard? Were they impervious to this scene? Or did they numb their feelings every night with drink to banish in temporary oblivion what they had done?

Was God in that camp, with prisoner and captor? Was God executed in the prisoner's pain? Was God crucified in the captor's cruelty?

'Who has believed our report
and to whom is the arm of the Lord revealed?..
He was despised and rejected by men
A man of sorrows and acquainted with grief

But he was wounded for our transgressions
He was bruised for our iniquities
The chastisement of our peace was upon him
And with his stripes we are healed
All we like sheep have gone astray
And the Lord has laid on him
The iniquity of us all
(Isaiah 53)

EASTER

A Pilgrimage to the Cross

It is only right that the final chapter in this book should lead both writer and reader to Easter. If scientists tell us that the world began with the extraordinary singularity we call the Big Bang about 15 billions years ago, then the gospel tells us that a new world we call the kingdom of God was brought into existence in one life, the life of Jesus Christ. Jesus' life was fulfilled and completed in the Easter event. Easter is God's spiritual and personal Big Bang.

1   THE ETERNAL NOW

We enter the holy season of Lent through the gateway of Ash Wednesday. This day is often called the 'day of ashes'. The ashes are obtained from burning the palms blessed on the previous Palm Sunday and are consecrated before the High Mass. The priest then marks the forehead of the worshipper with the ashes. This ceremony is derived from the custom of public penance dating back to the early Church. It is unknown at what date the practice was extended to include the whole congregation. We begin our seven-week pilgrimage to Easter Sunday.

Many issues are affecting our British way of life, bringing profound changes to this and succeeding generations. We cannot avoid these questions raised by these changing times. Surely what the British public needs, and so far has failed to receive, is powerful spiritual leadership from the established churches north and south of the border, with the exception, of course, of the Roman Catholic Church.

The British nation needs to return to God. This will not happen by using the worn-out forms of worship, and relying on old faith language. Nor will any positive changes be made through the age-old arguments used to persuade a sceptical public to believe in their form of denominational God. Rather, we need a radical re-discovery of the presence of God in society. We need a fundamental faith for a radical age. Current society must be challenged by the choice placed before it by of Blais Pascal's Wager in 'Les Pensées'.

'Either God is or he is not. But to which view shall we be inclined? Reason cannot decide this question. Infinite chaos separates us. At the far end of this infinite distance a coin is being spun which will come down heads or tails. How will you wager?... But you must wager There is no choice. You are already committed (because you are a living human being) **(Blais Pascall "Les Pensées" 418)**

During Lent let us re-examine our Christian credentials and renew our faith in the God and Father of Jesus Christ. Let us have the courage of our convictions to think deeply, even if these thoughts disturb us. What has happened to the Christian faith in many sections of society? Why does it appear so unattractive and of such little value? If Christianity in Britain is outwardly under threat, then inwardly the flames of faith have turned to ashes. Perhaps, if we rekindle our own faith, we may help others to discover Christianity, before this fading faith disappears altogether.

Paul Tillich taught in Union Theological Seminary after the 2nd World War. Born in Germany in 1886 he became a Lutheran pastor in 1912 and served as a military chaplain in the German Army during the 1st World War. He was traumatically affected by his war experiences. As a result his writings contain a strong political motivation for social reform and a major endeavour to mediate between the traditional Christian culture and an increasingly secularised society. A fierce critic of Hitler he was barred from teaching in German universities. He noted that he was the first non-Jewish academic 'to be so honoured'. He emigrated to America where he became a naturalised citizen in 1940. His sermons and writings are still relevant in our global situation. Tillich speaks of God's eternal presence .

In other words, despite being forgotten and denied, God is present in every age. In the face of bitter criticism against things spiritual, God's word still commands men and women to live moral lives according to God's will. In the contradiction of human conduct, which defies the ways of God, God's reign over the human race remains unchallenged. God's praise, like his presence, remains unaltered.

'Holy, holy, holy, Lord God of hosts
The whole earth is full of Thy glory'
(Isaiah 6.3)

Modern theological language must be both clear and bold. The present global scene for the families of nations is one of defiance against God. But God is still present, calling and seeking men and women. God is still patiently waiting for the human race to turn to God and walk in the ways of the Lord. Yet, despite all that is happening in the global scene the human race still defies God.

'I was ready to be sought by those who did not ask for me,
I was ready to be found by those who did not seek me,
I said, 'Here am I', 'Here am I '
To a nation that did not call on my name'
(Isaiah 65.1)

God will only be found in Jesus Christ. For our Lenten journey will take us unerringly to the crucified Christ of Calvary. The God we encounter is the God and Father of the crucified Christ. The question must be asked, Is the human race, prepared to encounter God in the cross of Calvary, and to hear God speak in the dying words of Jesus? Our destiny rests on our answer.

'I spread out my hands all the day to a rebellious people who walk in a way that is not good, following their own devices' **(Isaiah 65.2)**

2 THE INNER MYSTERY OF GOD

In Lewis Grassic Gibbons 'Sunset Song' the young Will Guthrie attended church regularly and every Sunday heard the preacher speak of Jehovah. He did not understand that this was the name of God. The name Jehovah fascinated him. He waited his chance to use that nice word. The opportunity arose when he was grooming the farm horse. Wanting the animal to move to the other side of the stall he smacked it on the rumps with the cry 'Move over Jehovah'. But he could not understand why John Guthrie his father punished and punched him so hard for using the name of God in vain. The name of God conveyed no meaning to the little boy. Now the gross ignorance of God and things Christian in the population at large is a disquieting feature in our modern society. In this generation the name of God often conveys no meaning at all. People are simply unaware of the experience of God, unconscious of God's presence, bereft of God's Word. In Lent we seek to re-discover and declare Christianity's true meaning. What does it mean to say that Jesus Christ the Son of God was crucified on the cross of Calvary for the sins of the world?

The Gospel of the crucified Christ is an incredible message. Roman crucifixion was brutal, reserved for slaves and criminals. For the Jews the cross was utterly repugnant, *'Cursed by God is the man who is hanged on a tree'* **(Deuteronomy 21.23).** For the Greeks the idea of a god dying as the Saviour of the world was utter folly. But this is the Easter message the world neither knows nor understands. *'We preach Christ crucified, a stumbling block to the Jews, and utter folly to the Greeks'* **(1 Corinthians 1. 21.25).**

But deeper still, at Easter, we encounter God. Easter is God's event, determined in God's will for our salvation and filled with God's grief at the suffering of his Son. Easter reveals the 'inner mystery of God' (Karl Rahner). The inner mystery is simply that our God has feelings. To appreciate this idea we must return to the Old Testament, to what John Calvin described as our teacher to help us understand the New. In the Old Testament God appears capricious. God is angry, and punishes his people to control their disobedience. But the heart of the Old Testament message is the clear revelation of the covenant God of Israel with compassion and feelings for his people. *'Like as a father pities his children, so the Lord pities those who fear him'* **(Psalm 103.13)**

From about 585-535 BC sections of the Jewish people were deported from Judea to Babylon. Demoralised and in a foreign land, they were a people who had lost sight of God. Our generation suffers the same plight. During that period the profound prophet Isaiah revealed to Israel the greatness of God's presence and the gentleness of God's heart. Isaiah taught the people that despite their terrible calamities their God remained faithful and true. Isaiah taught them how God's inner passion for their salvation overflowed in waves of compassion for their sufferings.

> 'My steadfast love shall not depart from you, and my covenant of peace shall not be removed, says the Lord who has compassion on you' **(Isaiah 54.10)**

This is Christianity's Easter message, undervalued by many, neglected by society. This is the God and Father of Jesus Christ who confronts us in the Easter event of his crucified Son. We encounter God in the cross, for global society is challenged by the will of God in the cross. The Christian faith is shaped by the Easter work of God. Here we see the eternal will and purpose of God for the salvation of men and women being accomplished. In the cross we encounter God the Father. Before the cross was created by the soldiers of the Roman Empire it was first created in the soul of God

The cross also reveals the 'inner mystery of God'. Not only is God to be found in the cross, but the cross is to be found in God. This is the inner mystery of God. God takes the pain and suffering of the cross into his very being, it can be said, into his heart and soul. The cross for crucifixion was fashioned from wood by Roman soldiers. But Calvary's cross of salvation was fashioned from love in the eternal life and saving will of God. The cross of salvation is the dialogue between Father and Son, sealed by the fellowship of the Holy Spirit. 'God showed his love towards us that while we were yet sinners Christ died for us' **(Romans 5.8).**

A Meditation

Melito of Sardis was a very early 2nd century Christian saint. He wrote these lovely words

> 'Nature trembled and said with astonishment,
> What new mystery is this?
> The judge is judged and remains silent
> The invisible one (God) is seen and does not hide himself
> The incomprehensible one is comprehended and does not resist
> The unmeasurable one is measured and does not resist
> The one beyond suffering suffers and does not avenge himself
> The immortal one dies and does not refuse death
> What new mystery is this?'

3 THE CROOKED TIMBER OF HUMANITY

*'Out of the crooked timber of humanity, no straight
thing can be made'* **(Immanuel Kant)**

Our Christian faith must be expressed radically, to meet the needs of contemporary society. We have seen the 'inner mystery of God', the pure passion of God for people. We encountered God in the cross. Christ was crucified unto salvation according to the will and purpose of God. But, in a profound way the cross was in the very heart of God. But the Easter cross of Christ acts as a mirror truly reflecting human nature. The cross reveals 'The crooked timber of humanity' (Immanuel Kant).

Human nature is a living contradiction. In the course of history the human race has created civilisation and filled it with wisdom, beauty and strength. But this same human race has been the author of despicable horrors. With our knowledge we can explore the very universe. Misused, that same knowledge can destroy all life. So, renewing nuclear weapons of mass destruction wastes resources and threatens world peace. Because the controlling presence of the Christian Gospel has been removed from society, we are witnessing excesses of violence and crime, and exaggerated deeds of immorality. This is the contradiction in human nature.

The human race has achieved great things. But the Bible tells us that human nature is subject to darkness and evil. The Bible calls this downward side of human nature by the name of 'sin'. This is the 'crooked timber of humanity' from which no straight things can come'. No one can deny that evil is rampant in human nature, and that sin does not dominate human conduct. Today's world is proof positive of the power of sin and evil. Primo Levi was an Italian Jew, who fought with the Italian resistance before he was captured and imprisoned in Auschwitz in 1943. Primo Levi soon realised that Auschwitz offered neither escape nor salvation. That is why 1.1 million people, 200,000 of them children, perished. Many lost sight of God, they saw *' no sacred face'* **(Primo Levi)**. The nations of the world before the days of Christ saw the faces of pagan idols, but never the sacred face of the one and only true God. Then one person walked across the face of the earth. His followers have forever called him Jesus the Saviour

because in Jesus we see the 'sacred face of God'
No-one has seen God at any time. The only Son, Jesus,
has revealed God to us **(John 1.18)**

In the years after the war many people questioned if it were possible to believe in a God of love and peace. Can there be a God of love after the war? But we ask another question. Can we still have faith in human nature – in the face of wars? Can we believe in the advancement of the human race? Will science and knowledge open the gateways to a purer and brighter future? Will the human race 'come of age' when it no longer needs the aid and support of God? Will men and women reach such a level of maturity that the Auschwitz and the Birkenau of past history will be absent from the future history of our children? Will the day ever dawn when Feuerbach and his disciples will be proved correct that humankind simply does not need God?

Or is history doomed to be the record of 'man's inhumanity to man'? (Robert Burns). Can we trust human nature? By the records of human deeds at individual and national levels the answer must be, albeit pronounced with deep regret, an emphatic 'No'. Humankind needs God. Not the apersonal God of the academic and philosopher, but the God and Father of Jesus Christ. The Christian gospel shows that human nature cannot be trusted to govern its life and direct its destiny. But God remains faithful to the human race. Because there is a 'Theology after the Cross', God acted in the crucified Christ, not to repair human nature, but to redeem and renew human nature. God straightened 'the crooked timber of humanity' (Kant) destroying sin and evil. So long as God is allowed into the human experience, allowed to be God in human nature, then the human spirit will never die. That was why, even in Auschwitz, the great *Shema* (*) of Israel and the Lord's Prayer of Christianity, were still repeated every day. This is our Easter faith in the crucified Christ. Let us declare this gospel message, trust our Christ, and worship our God.

'My steadfast love shall not depart from you
My covenant of peace shall not be removed,
Says the Lord who has compassion on you'
(Isaiah 54.10)

(*) *The Shema* **(Deuteronomy 6.4-9)** is the creedal statement repeated daily by every Jew

A   Meditation

Creator God
What is this contradiction that is man?
This man from the dust
     to rise, to aspire to be the very image of God
But the tree of knowledge
     Became the tree of cursing
Needing the tree of salvation, the cross
Only this contradiction in the very soul and being of man
     could transform an Eden into a wilderness
For the Lord walked through the creation of his love
     In the gentle breeze of the day
        to find nakedness covered with leaves
           innocence clothed with the rags of shame
    'What is man that you remember him,
    and the son of man that you visit him?' **(Psalm 8)**
Creator God
    You set him to have dominion over all creatures
    in their names to give them life
Thus was the creature in your own image
     made guardian of the creation of your hand

He was meant also to be his brother's keeper?
    but the blood of the slain rose up in protest and anguish
    for the brother became murderer
    the friend the foe, the fellow man a stranger
Thus has it continued from that first Eden day.

'Is this Man?'
Creator God
'In the beginning….'
Is this the man made in your image and formed by your love?
    'When I look to the heavens the work of your hands
    the sun, moon and stars which thou hast ordained..'
Now among these very constellations

feet walk where eyes could only see
    hands touch where minds could only conceive
'What is humankind to whom you gave dominion…'
    dominion but not destruction
    turning pruning hooks to spears
    forever learning the arts of war
    rocket, uranium,
    children's cries of fear and death
    buildings and bodies both burning
    fertile fields to harvest, killing fields of hate
Creator God willed a land flowing with milk and honey
    destructive man made a world flowing with blood
From the tree of life a sapling grew
    twisted and gnarled its branches
    the crooked timber of humanity
This is not man, of God's image
Made in the beginning to be like God

But, there once was a man,
    'who was the image of the invisible God,
    the first born of all creation' **(Colossians 1.15)**
    'In the beginning…. was the Word'
    'And the Word was with God
    And the Word was God
    The same was in the beginning with God
    All things were made by him
    And without him was not anything made that was made' **(John 1.1-4)**
Consider, for this is the true Man

4   THE LOVE OF GOD

During the first three Lenten studies we have thought on the abiding presence of God, the 'Eternal Now' **(Paul Tillich).** Then, we thought of our God and Father, of the 'inner mystery of God' as God takes the cross of our salvation into his own heart and soul. Then finally we thought about our human nature and how God had to renew the 'crooked timber of humanity' (Immanuel Kant). Now let us ponder how God renewed and straightened our human nature. *'God showed* *his love towards us that while we were yet sinners, Christ died for us'* **(Romans 5.8).**

Many years ago Highland fishermen made their own boats. My wife's forefathers in Kyle of Lochalsh practised that trade. At Lochcarron they felled the trees whose straight trunks provided the planks for the boat. But they also took black powder with them in to the forest, and with a careful explosion removed the roots from the ground. The natural curves in the roots would find a place in the construction of the boat. But, how was God to take the raw material of our human nature and shape it into his new humanity?

God achieved this through his renewing love. God showed his love towards us by carrying our sorrows. When God's pure nature and our broken nature met in Jesus only the love of God could make them one. Our loving God found many sorrows in human nature. Some sorrows we carry through our life. After they happened our life was permanently changed. It may have been the loss of a loved one or a child, an accident or illness. This has always been the cross of sorrow carried in our heart.

There once was a Man who lived in Galilee, and in Jesus our God and Father shared our grief, felt the pain of our heart, and carried our sorrows. But there is a profound difference. God takes our sorrow into his eternal soul, and grieves for them with an eternal passion. This is the love of God. When we love someone we open ourselves, with neither restraint nor protection, to his or her feelings and experiences. Such a love can be hurt, broken, crucified on the cross within the soul.

God was bruised when God showed his love towards us. For when the pure and holy God embraced broken human nature, then God's love went deeper. Loving God was hurt by something far more dangerous. God was bruised by our iniquities, *'God was wounded for our transgressions and bruised for our iniquities'* **(Isaiah 53.5).**

In a way we simply cannot know nor understand, our pure and holy God embraced all that is dark, evil and wrong in human life and history, including our own personal history. In this way God renewed human nature, and liberated people to fulfil their true humanity. So

169

Paul wrote, *'If anyone is in Christ he is a new person'* (**2 Corinthians 5.17**). But Paul also indicated the cost to God's love in making us new people. *'God made Jesus to be sin, Jesus who knew no sin that we might be made the righteousness of God in Him'* (**2 Corinthians 5.21**). Paul's language is dramatic, his thought courageous. In his love God made his Son our sin that we might become God's righteousness. Melito of Sardis described God's action in Jesus as 'the Royal Exchange'.

This is the 'unbearable burden' (Karl Barth) that Christ carried for us. The Christian gospel proclaims that God showed his love towards the world in this way. The Easter gospel tells the world how God in love embraced broken human nature. Let the world deride, we will honour God's name. Let the world scoff, we will marvel at what God has done. Man, look into your own heart and soul, for God is there, his grieving and bruised love seeking to embrace you. You say that you do not need God; God replies to you that he wants you. Feel the pulse beat of God's love from his broken heart. No matter how far you feel from God the arms of eternal love will embrace you. Threatening as the darkness around you has been, know that God shares your darkness and trembles in your fear. You are sore in mind and body, in his love God's wounds for you are eternal. *'God is love'* (**1 John 4.8**).

A Meditation on the Love of God

> *'God showed his love towards us that while we were yet sinners Christ died for us'* (**Romans 5.8**)

Gentle God
> You came to us as our Father in Jesus of Bethlehem
> In Jesus you walked the road of life from Nazareth to Calvary
> How else could you straighten the crooked timber of humanity
> > and dress us, the rough stones, to fit into Jesus,
> > the head cornerstone (**Mark 12.10**)

Gentle God' you showed your love towards us, you carried our sorrows
They came together in the embrace of your holy love
> your pure being and our broken human nature
What did that holy love find in your children?

a broken heart for the loss of loved ones
A discouraged spirit
the weight of life on wearied shoulders
A distressed soul,
saddened by its own faults and failings
But, Gentle God,
'You, the holy God, bore our grief and carried our sorrows'
(Isaiah 53.4).
What did that holy love find in your children?
a desire for greater things and a yearning to be better
In our mortal frame,
an eternal hope though dimmed still burning

But, Gentle God, provider for our needs,
'We esteemed you, despised and stricken,
rejected, a man of sorrows' **(Isaiah 53.3).**

Gentle God, *you were bruised for our iniquity* **(Isaiah 53.5)**
You found more in that 'crooked timber of humanity'
in the brokenness of your children
In your holy love you descended deeper into that brokenness
to find the fettered soul
In your radiance you penetrated evil's black and lifeless abode
and found benighted souls, captured people
Not by strength but through sacrifice
you sought to release them from bonds, dark and wrong,
too strong for their futile attempts to escape
'If anyone will rob the strong man's house, first bind the strong
man' **(Matthew 12.29)**
Gentle God, *you were wounded for our transgressions'*
(Isaiah 53.5)
In your holy love you allowed yourself to be bound and fettered
you were captured by the darkness caught by the wrong.
Gentle God, 'You showed your love towards us…'
These things you did for us in Jesus
What an 'unbearable burden' you placed on his great soul
for Jesus was pure but was made soil-ed
honourable but suffered shame

Your Son was sovereign but became our servant
    'God made Jesus to be sin who knew no sin' **(2 Corinthians 5.21)**
    'The living One he made his grave with the dead'
    'The righteous One his resting place with the wicked'
    'He descended into hell'
    'The Righteousness of God'
    'That we might be the righteousness of God in him'
    (2 Corinthians 5.21)
Gentle God, 'You showed your love towards us…'
    'That we might be the righteousness of God in him'
See how your kind love directs our gaze
    towards Jesus, crucified One
Watch as the finger of the hand of love
    point out to our seeking eyes
    the wounds he bore,
'Tis the gospel story of God
Father God
We bow humbly to honour God, to acknowledge God, to cleave to God
Gentle God
We look into heart and soul,
    there is much to disturb and distress
But look further, soul within me!
See your God!
Meet your Jesus!
Feel within you God's love through your Jesus
For *'God is Love'* **(1 John 4.8)**

5   CHRIST'S COMPASSION

We have reached the fifth stage in our Lenten pilgrimage. From this point we move to Palm Sunday when we will remember Christ's entry into Jerusalem. Thereafter our Lord Jesus will go to the cross through Holy Week. The fifth Sunday in Lent is called Passion Sunday. 'Passion' describes our profound emotions. When we feel for someone then we show com-passion. During Lent we want to declare boldly the true meaning of our Christian faith.

    In the Gospel of Matthew 8-9 we find a collection of ten acts of healing carried out by Jesus together with three confrontational incidents when Jesus is challenged about his conduct. These two chapters are summarised in **Matthew 9.35-38.** One verse crystallises Jesus' com-passion, his fellow-feeling, for the people. *'When Jesus saw the crowds he had compassion for them, for they were harassed and helpless like sheep without a shepherd'.* The Greek word used for compassion is 'splagchnizomai', and expresses the deepest emotions that anyone could feel for another person. On Passion Sunday we reflect on a few scenes from Jesus' ministry where his compassion is revealed. In all of these scenes from Jesus' ministry the same Greek verb describes Jesus' deep feelings. One translation reads, 'Jesus was filled with tenderness'. Jesus was terribly upset.

A Meditation

'Jesus touch these blinded eyes that he can see' **(Mark 8.22-26)**
'Now what do you see', the Saviour asked
'I see but with difficulty', he replied
'I see men but they look like trees walking'
Then the act of mercy, Saviour Christ
  when your healing became your passion
  and his wholeness came but only through your sacrifice
Jesus, you cared passionately,
  he saw clearly

> *'A father with a broken son cried out, 'Jesus I believe in you but mend my broken faith, heal my son, have compassion on us'* **(Mark 9. 17-27).**

Jesus, we watch, we feel, we tremble, for something beyond us
  takes place.
The heart-broken, pain-filled compassion of a father for a son
  yearning for healing fuses as one with the heart-felt, God-
  made-pure, compassion of Jesus to heal
At that very moment healing became saving
Jesus, in that father's anguish for his little son, did you feel the
  eternal yearning of God your Father for his children?
Jesus, did you then know that healing must become saving,
  and saving could be found only in the cross?

But Jesus the compassion of your soul was seared by a terrible
  pain, like the spear of the cross thrust towards your heart
  and twisted in your pierc-ed side
For in these days of healing you were misunderstood even by the
  one who came closest to you.
  *'Behold the Lamb of God who takes away the sins of the
  world'* **(John 1.29).**
Doubted you,
  'Are you the coming one or do we look for another?'
  (Matthew 11.1-3).
  'Go tell John what you hear and see' **(Matthew 11.4).**

Jesus, what more could you have done to show who you were and
why you had come among us? Your words were sad, for then you
knew they all misunderstood you. Misunderstanding led to betrayal,
betrayal opened the way to the cross.
Jesus, on Passion Sunday we remember your com-passion for us all

6   PALM SUNDAY – THREE DONKEYS

On Palm Sunday we remember Jesus' entry into Jerusalem at the
start of these eight most holy days of Easter. To understand Easter
we must march with the crowd behind Jesus on that fateful Sunday of
palm leaves. In the Western Church Palm Sunday is considered the
first day of Holy Week, and its services convey a sense of foreboding
as the worshippers enters into these holy days that lead inexorably to
Good Friday. By contrast in the orthodox Eastern Church Palm
Sunday is not included in Holy Week, but rather is regarded as a
joyous festival remembering Christ's triumphal entry. Bethphage,
from where Jesus entered Jerusalem, was situated on the Mount of
Olives. Every Jew knew the significance of this location. On the last
day of judgment God would stand on the Mount of Olives to judge the
world **(Zechariah 14.4).**   Three times over Jesus had warned his
disciples of this moment **(Mark 8.31-33; 9.30-32; & 10.32-34).** We will
be struck by the resolute lines etched across his countenance. *'When
the days* (of his passion) *drew near Jesus set his face to go to
Jerusalem'* **(Luke 9.51).**   The secret of Palm Sunday is revealed
through the stories of three donkeys.

A stark contradiction marks Jesus' entry into Jerusalem on that first Palm Sunday.

Did his entry stop the busy city?   Did the people wait with bated breath, as God's divine drama unfolded before them? Or was this an insignificant 'non-event' drawing only passing glances from passers-by?   John Calvin captures this contradiction.

'To claim royal honour Christ entered Jerusalem riding on an ass. Magnificent splendour indeed!   Add that the ass was borrowed for the occasion, and lacking saddle and trappings, the disciples threw their clothes across it. All this a sign of terrible shame and poverty. A great crowd followed him. But who were they, the poor and despised masses. It seemed as if Christ exposed himself deliberately to mockery' **(John Calvin)**

Jesus' entry to Jerusalem was the arrival of the Royal Saviour. When a king entered a city on a humble donkey, he demonstrated that he came in peace, on a mission of good will. An aggressor would ride on a war-horse.   Jesus is the royal Saviour bringing peace and salvation.   That is why the Early Church realised that Jesus had fulfilled the great Old Testament prophecy,

'Rejoice greatly, O daughter of Zion!
Shout aloud, O daughter of Jerusalem!
Lo, your king comes to you, triumphant and victorious is he
Humble riding on an ass, on a colt the foal of an ass
(Zechariah 9.9)

In acting in this way Jesus openly declared that he came with the regal authority of God to establish God's kingdom. The spectators realised that Jesus was declaring himself the Messiah of God, but they little anticipated what would follow. So, it was natural for them to shout. *'Blessed be the King who comes to save us in the name of the Lord'* **(Luke 19.28-40, especially verse 38. See   Psalm 118.26-27).**

But the Saviour of God's people was a humble Saviour.   So a donkey brought Jesus the King into Jerusalem. There is a lovely poem about that scene,

'When fishes flew and forests walked, and figs grew upon thorn,
Some moment when the moon was blood, then surely I was born.
With monstrous head and sickening cry, and ears like errant wings,

The devil's walking parody on all four-footed things.
Fools, for I also had my hour, one far fierce hour and sweet,
There was a shout about my ears, and palms before my feet'
(G. K. Chesterton 'The Donkey')

The picture of the humble animal carrying the gentle Jesus teaches us a deeper truth about our Lord. Jesus came as the humble Saviour. In this way the poor and despised were encouraged to come to Jesus. Jesus scorned wealth, power, and possessions. Setting aside his royal power as the Son of God Jesus came to ordinary people to preach the Good News of the kingdom of heaven. Jesus still enters our life as the humble Saviour. In this way Jesus reveals to us 'the human face of God' (Bishop John Robinson). Or, as Karl Barth wrote, Jesus shows us 'the humanity of God'. God comes to us in the utter humanity of Jesus, bringing us forgiving love, healing mercy, and infinite grace. This movement of God for our salvation is clearly described in the second story about a donkey, the parable of the Samaritan who placed the injured traveller on his own beast **(Luke 10.29-37)**. As the Good Samaritan rescued that broken man from the dust, God stoops low to gather up broken people in his sweeping act of salvation.

Jesus came from Bethany to Calvary. Braving the crowd a group of women watched Jesus slowly proceed to the temple. One of these women was Mary of Nazareth. She was the mother of Jesus. As she watched her son Mary remembered that journey on a donkey from Nazareth to Bethlehem **(Luke 2.1-7)**. Bethlehem scenes appeared before her as if from yesterday. Anxious Joseph on that weary journey, he never did recover his old self after that journey, somehow brought her husband to an early grave. The first sight of Bethlehem, the full houses and closed doors, the track to the stable, the repugnant smell from the animals, the coarse straw, the crude manger, the rough shepherds, the three strange travellers, her child so helpless in such poverty. So mused Mary, thus can we meditate that poverty was the place of his birth, wretchedness the scene of his living, and shame the final outcome of this journey. Is this, *'Glory to God in the highest, on earth peace and goodwill'?* **(Luke 2.14)**.

A Meditation

In humility, uncompromising humbleness
Great Saviour, you come to us
We make for you a comfortable home
    but you pass it by to find a manger rude and bare
'Take no thought for your life, for food or home' **(Matthew 6.25)**
Jesus, that lesson you taught us, that lesson you lived
    in uncompromising humility you did not spare yourself
    in undiminished humbleness you spared us
We erect a throne
    but you ascend a cross
Deep the colours of our garland of flowers
    deeper still the red from your crown of thorns.
By your words we are taught
    but by your stripes we are healed
Jesus you do not need to die we will change for the better
    but you did die and we are changed forever

7 HOLY WEEK

Monday

On this day we remember how Jesus cleansed the courts of the temple and declared his Father's house to be a house of prayer for all the nations.

In his day (about 600.BC) the people did not heed Jeremiah's dire warnings that they were living contrary to God's will **(Jeremiah 7.1-15).** They had Solomon's great temple to assure them of God's presence and blessing.   In the temple built by Herod Jesus found moneychangers and sellers of sacrificial animals making the temple appear like a bazaar **(Mark 11.12-26).** Let Jesus enter the temple of our soul and cleanse it, as he did the temple.

Tuesday

On the Tuesday of Holy Week we are taught by the parables of Jesus. We learn from a group of parables deep in meaning, demanding in decision, the parable of the wicked husbandmen **(Mark 12.1-12).** A group of five parables is contained in **Matthew 24.32 – 25.46**. The most severe is the parable of the Last Judgment, the sheep and the goats. In Holy Week we need to remember that there is a day of reckoning - for everybody.

Wednesday

On Wednesday in Holy Week we remember how Christ remained alone in Bethany, preparing himself for coming ordeal **(Mark 14.1-11).** A woman with an alabaster jar of precious nard broke open the jar and poured the costly ointment over his head. This act of wholesome generosity was her response to the complete self-giving she had seen in Jesus **(Mark 14.1-11).**   Let our response to Christ be full and complete. With warmth and affection let us renew our dedication to our Saviour

Thursday

On the Thursday we remember how our Lord washed the disciples feet in utter humility **(John 13.1-11).** Jesus celebrated the Passover meal with his disciples **(Matthew 26.17-19).** During the Meal Jesus instituted the holy Sacrament **(Matthew 26.26-29).** Jesus then gave the disciples the great words of comfort and peace **(John 14-16)**. Knowing that Judas was ready to betray him **(Matthew 26.20-25),** Jesus went into the darkness and agony of the Garden of Gethsemane where he was captured **(Matthew 26. 36-55).** Jesus suffered thus for you and I. We cannot fathom the depth of Jesus' agony.

Good Friday

There followed a night of indescribable torture and torment from Thursday evening till Friday morning. Jesus went on trial before the high priest, Herod, and twice before Pilate. Jesus was brutally tortured **(Mark 15.16-19).** At 6 o'clock on Friday morning, weakened, in extreme pain, and with a ring of thorns piercing his head Jesus was led to Calvary carrying the cross piece. At 9 o'clock in the morning (the third hour of the day) Jesus was nailed by his hands to the cross piece, and by his feet to the upright. At 12 noon (the sixth hour of the day) the whole world was darkened. At 3.o'clock in the afternoon (the ninth hour) Jesus died **(Matthew 27. 32-50)**

'Is it nothing to you all ye who pass by?
Look and see if there be any sorrow like unto my sorrow,

which was brought upon me, which the Lord inflicted
on the day of his fierce anger' **(Lamentations 1.12)**
We call this day 'Good Friday'
Were you there when they crucified my Lord?
'There is a green hill far away outside the city wall'

A Meditation

A singularity they call it (*)
    A nano second with all time and space
        All energy, life and light
            Gas and element, matter with mass
    A diminished second so swift
        That the blink of the eye is longer than eternity
One moment so special
    that the vast universe found its life
        the stars their light
            and the rules created by which they moved
In the world's wisdom it is called a bang
    A big One
Good Friday
    a spiritual singularity
        in the vast reaches of the universe
            through the gigantic stretches of billions of years
One planet among the billions of billions
    One person since the origin of species
        One nation since cave dweller to temple worshipper
One place called the cross
    one day timed Good Friday
        one Person - Jesus
One event
Jesus, the Son of God, died
    In a spiritual black hole
        Trapping all life within its bourne
            Bending all light into darkness
GOD DIED

(*) A singularity is the name given by astronomers to that split-second moment when the Big Bang took place about 15 billion years ago, from which our entire universe evolved.   We can describe Easter as God's spiritual singularity from which the Kingdom of God like a new universe came forth.   Easter is God's spiritual Big Bang.

Saturday

Joseph of Arimathea and Nicodemus removed our Lord's broken body and laid him in a tomb **(John 19.38-42)**. By oppression and judgment was Jesus taken away **(Isaiah 53.8)**. Jesus made his grave with the wicked **(Isaiah 53. 9).**

> *'Jesus died for sins once and for all, the righteous for the unrighteous, being put to death in the flesh but made alive in the spirit. Jesus preached to the spirits in prison, in death'*
> **(1 Peter 3.18-22)**

Between Good Friday and Easter Sunday nestles the Saturday of Holy Week.

A Meditation

That Saturday, after Good Friday,
    was the Sabbath day of rest
    the first day of Passover.
Sabbath is the day of rest
    what was 'rest' for the Lamb of God
    who took away the sins of the world?

The Sabbath day of rest
    'The Lord rested the seventh day after his creation' **(Genesis 2.2)**
You had made for us a new creation
    In Christ the new Adam **(1 Corinthians 15.45)**
    Then, Gentle God,
    What was that rest in these hours 'tween cross and empty tomb
    The rest of sorrow, the repose of sacrifice

The Sabbath day of rest
    'The Lord rested the seventh day and made it holy' **(Genesis 2.3)**
The Sabbath day was still an holy day **(Exodus 20.8)**
    What was your holiness
        that presided over these hours

'tween cross and empty tomb
What have you done to your holiness?
You have made it saving grace
Holy, holy, holy
Gentle God of the cross
Heaven and earth are full of your mercy
Glory be to God bent low.

8   48 HOURS

*'On the cross God stretched out his hands to embrace
the ends of the earth'*
(Cyril of Jerusalem)

Paul Tillich recounts his conversation with a Jewish friend about Jesus Christ. From their separate perspectives they shared both differences and agreements. But when they thought of the 48 hours from the dawn of Good Friday till the dawn of Easter Sunday they faced a fundamental and irreconcilable difference. For Christianity's unique difference from Judaism, for that matter from every other religion, was these 48 hours. The Christian gospel declares that at Easter God saved the world with his own life in Christ.   Or, as Cyril of Jerusalem wrote, 'On the cross God stretched out his hands to embrace the ends of the earth'

A Meditation

Gentle God
What happened in these hours?
we do not ask only wonder
From your holiness was born saving grace
but that holiness was pained as in child birth
holiness the womb in which grace was conceived
holiness the handmaid of the Lord
What happened in that space
where the Arimathean laid the Christ
We do not come close to this place
nor touch its border **(Exodus 19.12-13)**
Not a ladder reaching to heaven **(Genesis 28.12)**
but a cross stooping down from heaven

THE COMPASSION OF CHRIST

This day, this space
Between cross and empty tomb
They belong to God

9 THE RESURRECTION

'If the resurrection is cut out then we have no religion left,
no assurance of faith left, in fact no faith left at all'
("Commentary on 1 Corinthians" 15. 20)

This is the way John Calvin highlights the importance of the resurrection. If there is no Easter resurrection then there is simply no Christianity at all. Without the two-fold event of Easter we have no faith. Christianity is the Easter faith in the Easter Christ believed in by the Easter people of the Easter God. If our faith is not thus founded then that faith is certainly not Christianity. If we believe in any other Jesus apart from the Easter Jesus then we have yet to meet the Jesus of the gospel, nor meet him where he promises to come to us, at Calvary's cross, and with Mary at the empty tomb **(John 20. 11-18)**.

Easter Sunday is filled with the glory to God. This is the day of the resurrection. Truly Jesus died upon the cross, no physical frame ever survived crucifixion. But, that God raised Jesus from the dead is the foundation stone of the Christian faith. The resurrection is the Christian gospel. 'It (the resurrection) is the first and last and dominating element in the Christian consciousness of the New Testament' **(James Denney "Studies in Theology" page 49)**.

Jesus appeared to Mary **(John 20. 11-18)**, walked to Emmaus with two disciples **(Luke 24. 13 ff)**, and came to the eleven disciples **(John 20.19-23 and 21)**. These were real people and real events. The New Testament described the crucifixion of Jesus in minute detail. But the New Testament never described the resurrection of Jesus. The Gospels accounts tell of Peter and John finding the Empty Tomb **(John 20.1-10)**. While Paul quotes the tradition of the Early Church, *'I delivered to you what I have received, that Christ died for our sins, that he was buried, that he was raised the thirds day'* **(1 Corinthians 15.3-4)**. But that is as far as it goes because that uniquely supreme event in the whole of human history belongs entirely to God. *'The crucifixion* *is the beginning of our salvation and the resurrection is its completion'* **(John Calvin "Commentary on 1st Corinthians" 15.20)**

The Resurrection in God

During Lent we spoke of the 'inner mystery of God', how the cross was in God. We spoke of the suffering of the Son being answered by the grief of the Father. We spoke of God taking the cross into his very being and giving us his life in pure and holy love. But at Easter we wonder yet more deeply. Because if the cross lies in the inner life of God, so too does the resurrection of our Lord. The death and resurrection of Jesus in time and history were cherished from all eternity in the inner life of God. They are the 'inner mysteries of God'. For the cross in God tells of God's grief, but the resurrection in God speaks of God's life and hope, peace and joy

On Good Friday the grief of God the Father responded to the agony of God the Son, likewise with the resurrection. The resurrection lies cradled in the life and love of God the Father for his Son in the intimacy of the Spirit. By his own life and love God the Father raised up from the dead Jesus Christ. *'This Jesus God raised up'* **(Acts 2.32.).** As Paul wrote **(I Corinthians 15.20)**

'Now in fact Christ has been raised from the dead' – by God

God in the Resurrection

So we encounter God in the resurrection. From the grief of God in the cross is born the hope and joy of God in the empty tomb. As God took death into his very being on the cross, so from that death God brought life to us in the resurrection. Nay, more, it was not the old life subject to decay, but a new life beyond decay. So, Paul could declare, *'If anyone is in Christ he is a new person, the old has passed away, behold all things are become new'* **(2 Corinthians 5. 17).** This is because Jesus 'is' that new life. Jesus is the resurrection and the life. *'I am the resurrection and the life, he who believes in me though they were to die, 'yet shall they live'* **(John 11.25).** This saying teaches two great lessons. Firstly, it is a description of Jesus, *'I am the resurrection and the life'.* Secondly, it tells us of the relationship between Jesus and the believer, *'The one who believes in me shall*

183

never die'. Both lessons apply to the Christian life, because in the resurrection, the rising of Jesus Christ, we encounter God. Believers are enlivened by God's life, and raised to a new life by the same power of God which raised Jesus from the dead. This is the immense lesson taught by St. Paul **(Romans 6.1-11).**

The Joy Of Easter

This is the Easter gospel, in which we trust, whose message we proclaim.

The Easter resurrection is the key to unlock the door to new life. It is the foundation upon which we can stand, and standing firm can face the world. The Easter gospel is the hope, not to be disappointed, ' ... *that neither death nor life, nor height nor depth, nor any other creature shall be able to separate us from the love of God found in Christ Jesus our Lord and Saviour'* **(Romans 8.38-39).** May the God and Father of Jesus Christ bless you this happy Easter time. May you feel a deep inner renewal of faith. May the real Easter message thrill and encourage you. You are the Easter people trusting the Easter Christ. As John Calvin wrote, *'The crucifixion is the beginning of our salvation and the resurrection is its completion'. 'This is the day that the Lord has made, let us rejoice in it and be glad'* **(Psalm 118.24).**

The Resurrection for the Believer

The events of Easter took place. There was a time and place in human history when Jesus Christ was crucified on a Roman cross at Calvary. But, equally real, in time, place and history Jesus Christ was raised from the dead. Both events occurred in time, because both events were effected by God. Many scholars doubt the reality of the resurrection, and seek to rationalise it. I believe such ideas are misguided. The resurrection is real because it is the work of God. That is why the Christian gospel is the message of the death and resurrection of Jesus. After Peter and John left her at the empty tomb Mary met Jesus. Mary recognised the Lord when Jesus spoke her name, *'Mary'* **(John 20.11-18).**

When Jesus calls us by our own name then we know that the resurrection is real. Look at it this way. For over forty years as a minister I entered the homes of bereaved families who had lost a loved one. They sought comfort in their mourning and an assurance that their loved one was 'safe in the arms of Jesus'. Such families, your family, did not want spurious theories about how the resurrection could be explained. They wanted to hear the ringing conviction of the gospel,

'As Christ was raised from the dead by the glory of God
we too will walk in newness of life' **(Romans 6.4).** *Because, 'The fact*
is, Christ has been raised from the dead' **(1 Corinthians 15.20)**

A Meditation

GOD LIVES – THE RISING
The rising of God from God
    to God within God
Within the spiritual blackness of dying
From dying springs living
    for living is stronger than dying
From blackness shines light
    for the light shines and darkness is consumed
From nothingness arises creation, new creation,
    re-creation, undying people
Our origin evolved from many species
Our goal a new humanity
Resurrection people
    forever living within finite life
    never dying
A star shone over the first Bethlehem
    the divine into the human
New stars surge from the second Bethlehem
    the human into the divine
Bethlehem of the empty tomb
    Where we are born again
Resurrection
    New stars in recreated lives
        Galaxies of blessings
            The universe we call
                The Kingdom of God

Postscript

I would like to add one word in conclusion. Every time I go to London I make a point of going to St. Paul's cathedral. After I spend some time in that magnificent edifice I then make my way down a narrow and short side street. Few frequent this little area dwarfed as it is by the mighty St. Paul's. There I find a little old fashioned building. Around the top of the four walls in bold lettering a foot high a verse from Scripture has been painted in Latin. The verse reads

'But far be it for me to glory except in the cross of our Lord Jesus Christ, by which the world has been crucified unto me, and I to the world' **(Galatians 6.14).**

In company with countless millions who have run, or are running, the race of faith looking unto Jesus the author and finisher of their faith, that verse means everything to me.

The Christian faith gives me the chance to mould my world by the shape of the cross, and see people in the light of the resurrection. When I was a minister in a charge during the busy winter months, I used to study a subject as far removed from my professional reading as a theologian. In this way I kept my reading balanced. This was the way I became interested in astronomy and cosmology. I sought to keep my mind open to the wider world of scientific thought and discovery in order that my faith could be at home in these worlds. In this way I developed a deep personal desire to embrace with the Christian faith the worlds of science and philosophy, the arena of human activity, and the theatre of artistic expression in music and art.

We live in the country. The other night with our grandchildren we went to look for the moon. As they directed their bright torches at the moon they asked, 'Will they see us from the moon?' They are already reaching out to embrace this wonderful world.

If I were to write a little letter to my grandchildren and their generation it would read

'Dear children,

You are growing up into a world that confronts you with many challenges but also contains many wonders. Resist these things that would lower your quality of life, hold fast to everything that is good

You will meet many people who think they are rich because of what they hold in their hands. But often the truly valuable things in life are not seen, they are kept in our heart. They are trust and love, kindness and loyalty.

You will meet others who will seek to persuade you that this wonderful world can be understood through their learning and discoveries. They believe this world can be examined and somehow explained away. They have much to teach us, but there is so much more to life than their discoveries. Do not be misled by such people. For this world in which you grow up is richer beyond measure, and contains more surprises yet to be discovered.

There are so many ways to experience the happiness and pleasure of growing up.

One such way that I have found helpful is to share your life with God. God was not up there in the sky when you shone your torches at the moon. God was right beside you at our house. God was with you in Jesus

You see, Jesus lives in this life. He will help you understand what is right and wrong. He helps develop all your abilities, he gives you something to live for, a goal in life. Jesus is in the classroom, the university, the place where you will work. Jesus listens to your music, and laughs with you when you have fun. Jesus helps you to overcome disappointments, and to avoid moral dangers. Jesus is not just in the church, he is at home in your world, and the world belongs to him. Enjoy your life to the full, dear children.'

Rev Tom